Gordon Ramsay
Cooking for Friends

Cook's notes

I suggest seasoning with good-quality sea salt and freshly ground pepper, and using fresh herbs for best flavour.

Spoon measures are level (unless otherwise specified): 1 tsp is equivalent to 5ml; 1 tbsp is equivalent to 15ml.

Use large eggs (unless otherwise specified), ideally organic or free-range. If you are pregnant or in a vulnerable health group, avoid dishes using raw or lightly cooked eggs.

Oven timings are for fan-assisted ovens. If using a conventional oven, increase the temperatures by 15°C (1 gas mark). Individual ovens may vary in actual temperature by 10°C from the setting, so it is important to know your oven. One way to do this is to use an oven thermometer to check your oven's accuracy.

Timings are provided as guidelines, with a description of colour or texture where appropriate, but readers should rely on their own judgement as to when a dish is properly cooked.

HarperCollins*Publishers*
77–85 Fulham Palace Road,
Hammersmith, London W6 8JB
www.harpercollins.co.uk

First published by HarperCollins*Publishers* 2008
This edition published in 2011

© Gordon Ramsay 2008
Photographs © Ditte Isager 2008

The author asserts the moral right to be
identified as the author of this work

A CIP catalogue record of this book is
available from the British Library

ISBN 978-0-00-738278-1

Printed and bound in China by
South China Printing Ltd.

Gordon Ramsay
Cooking for Friends

Food **Mark Sargeant**
Text **Emily Quah**
Photographer **Ditte Isager**
Stylist **Christine Rudolph**
Art Director **Patrick Budge**

HarperCollins*Publishers*

Contents

Introduction

As a chef, I work at a thousand miles an hour, but when I'm at home, I want to slow down. I leave my chef's jacket at work, and I walk into a domestic setting, where everything is completely different. At home, our kitchen is family-run, and it's a relaxed place. A lot of people see cooking as a chore, but we bring an element of fun into it. For me, it's a therapy, and it's happening more and more that I cook with Tana and the children, especially Megan, my oldest. The kitchen is open-plan, with a large sofa and space to unwind. The focus is on the stove, which was built in Paris. It needed a concrete plinth as its foundation, to carry the weight, and after it was installed, the kitchen was built around it. The stove has a chrome-faced, water-cooled frontage so the kids can't burn themselves while they slice spring onions or grate fresh parmesan.

I can't sit at home with my feet up, reading the newspaper. But having said that, I am beginning to learn about being calm. Everyone always imagines that it must be hectic in the Ramsays' kitchen, but it's not. We turn cooking into serious fun. To an extent, everything we do is spontaneous. We're very lucky in that we have some great farmers' markets nearby. The kids will go and buy cheese, fresh organic chicken, and a selection of the farmers' vegetables. They become totally involved in the shopping, putting aside a percentage of their pocket money for good measure. They love that.

You get a young child to pay for a kilo of turnips or carrots, and then see how excited they are about what's on the plate later. They get pocket money according to age. Megan's nine, so she's on £9. The twins, Holly and Jack, are on £8, and Tilly is on £6. They all wait for their birthdays because they know they'll get a pound increase. They are learning that in order to live well and have a healthy lifestyle, they've got to eat well. If they never pursue cooking as a career, that's not going to upset me. I just need to know that they can fend for themselves in the kitchen.

The naughtiest child on the day gets to do the washing-up. Whoever's not on washing-up duty will set the table. We do have a dishwasher, but it's rarely used, unless we've got a big party going on in the garden. I think the kids need to know what it's like to wash up. When I was a child, we had a cleaning rota at home. I didn't grow up with dishwashers and everything being done for you. As four children, we were all involved, and Mum managed a strict rota, so no one escaped their turn at the washing-up, even though we had busy lives: me with my football and the others with their music.

I'm a bit old-fashioned in this way. I don't have rules and regulations at home, but what I do have is a very hands-on family. It's not me standing there, cooking away and everyone watching. On Saturday morning, after the girls have been to the gym and Jack has got back from football, we come back and prepare a late lunch together. We won't eat dinner until seven thirty, eight o'clock, and then it will be a slow braise. For

Sunday lunch, we have friends and family round, and over the weekend, we might indulge in a dessert. On Monday to Friday, it's a substantial main course, followed by fruit.

Not everything comes from the farmers' market. It would be great, but just not practical. Tana will shop two or three times a week at a supermarket, and I have to say that some of the supermarkets are doing some really good, interesting food lines. Out of respect for real quality ingredients, we also go to specialist purveyors, like Randalls, our butchers. Knowing where your food comes from and being able to trace it right back to its source is important to me.

I'd rather spend more and eat less, buy the best quality ingredients and savour them, buy what we need and no more. Sometimes I find it embarrassing when I see the amount of food that we, as a nation, waste.

I find it frustrating at how we are forgetting that there has always been a traditional British cuisine, and it doesn't have to revolve around steak and kidney pie, or fish and chips. I remember watching my mother cook at the Cobweb tearooms in Stratford-upon-Avon, making ham hock barley soup, white veal stew, the most amazing honey-glazed roast ham, and, of course, all served with chips. What you don't see nowadays is the way she used to stud the ham with cloves and caramelize it. All that forgotten, unfashionable stuff was traditionally British. Wonderful, but forgotten in our haste to experiment with modern fads.

We are at risk of trying to make food too sophisticated as we move along, changing ingredients to follow what's in vogue. The words 'trendy food', 'trendy restaurants' and especially 'trendy chef' make me cringe. It is not always necessary to use foie gras with the finest fillet steak and line-caught turbot. Sometimes it's just better to braise some oxtail and cook with mackerel, pollack or gurnard.

I'm always excited around food. There are so many opportunities to prepare and eat good food in the home if you have the patience and determination. Once you've got good at making amazing fresh pasta, you will want to make ravioli. Once you've mastered the perfect ravioli, you will want to get more intricate with the filling. A domestic kitchen is a far superior place to what it was ten years ago. And we're competitive as a nation. We want to outdo our neighbours. We know and understand the importance of eating well, so mix that with our natural peacock tendency to be the one who hosts the best dinner parties, and you are on the path to a whole new dimension in your life at home.

But don't get overconfident and miss the point when preparing a dinner party. Lighten up, have a glass of wine. Have your guests in the kitchen with you, and instead of showing off to them, involve them. Delegate the starter and the dessert while you tend to the main course. What can be difficult for me when going to dinner parties is when people hang on your every forkful. The food has been prepared in order to be enjoyed. It should be relaxing, not there to take you into a stress zone.

The palate can be educated. It's a matter of learning, of discipline and of practice. It is also the best reason in the world to stop smoking. Smoking will always dull your palate and confuse your taste buds. It's a bit like playing football with your laces tied together.

I love to see an array of cookbooks on someone's shelf so that I can see who excites people. And I love to see a top chef's recipes domesticated for home use. I have hundreds of cookbooks, though slightly fewer now, after taking all of our Delia cookbooks to Oxfam. I was astonished when I saw her using canned mince. Where's the feel-good factor in that sort of compromise? It just gives the wrong message. We're one of the hardest-working nations in the world. We move forwards, not backwards. The phenomenal confidence that Delia gave people, the impact that she has had over thirty years, has to my mind been shattered in one book. It made me quite distraught and taught me never to invest in a football club, if that's what it does to you.

I get nervous if people tell me that they follow my recipes word for word. A recipe is a guideline. Adding, subtracting, evolving it – that is part of the pleasure. If a particular herb is not to your taste, if you don't like the strength of rosemary, say, by all means, use thyme, especially lemon thyme. If you prefer the purple basil in the middle of summer, then great (if you ever can get it). If you are not excited about using swede the way I am, then use celeriac. We don't eat enough turnips or kohlrabies – in terms of flavour, they're extraordinary. Adapting the

ingredients is completely in your hands. But the method is what matters. The techniques in cooking are rigorous and imperative: they are your passport to a successful dish. Cooks must practise, practise, practise. Anyone can learn, but you need focus, proper understanding, and to go at the right pace, not running before you can walk.

I'll never forget, as a 22-year-old commis chef, working for the Roux brothers, all I wanted to do was bake, make the most amazing puff pastry, choux pastry, sourdough bread, and tomato and olive bread, using a natural yeast and fermentation. As a baker, you would start at midnight and work until midday. At half past midnight, it fell silent. All you could hear was the timers and the steamers for the second proof. On one occasion, I had to put together this marquise chocolate. Pascal, the young French pastry chef I was taking the section over from, could hardly speak English. He left me a box of After Eight mints, and said that I was to put a layer of chocolate mousse in the bottom of the mould and then add the After Eights. He wanted me to cut them in half and arrange them in threes in order to get this line of mints going through the mousse. I was thinking: this guy's winding me up. He's trying to get me into trouble. So I ate the mints instead.

The next day, Albert Roux came in. You have to give him one of everything, down to every bread roll, so that he can taste it all. I gave him the marquise, and he went bananas because it didn't have the mints running through the centre. I couldn't believe he would make an amazing chocolate mousse and stick After Eight mints in the middle. I got a bollocking. It got thrown in the bin, and I had to start again. I grew up on a council estate, but trained with the best. I've trained my palate with some of the greatest chefs, but sometimes you have to question the best. Cookery is quite a journey. Take nothing for granted.

Gordon Ramsay

hot and cold
soups

Soups are truly versatile: they can be as light or substantial as you want. In small amounts, a good soup can excite the palate in the form of a starter. Enrich the broth or bulk it up with chunky ingredients and it converts into a satisfying main course.

I fell in love with chowders when I spent a few months filming in America. We tasted amazing New England clam chowders on the East Coast. In San Francisco, one of the main treats was sourdough bread bowls filled with thick bisques and creamy soups. Once you've devoured the soup, you're left with a flavourful bread bowl to break apart and savour. Whether you're making an elegant blended soup or a more homely chowder, always start with a good base. Good-quality stock provides a depth of flavour that brings together all the elements in a soup. It is also important to season well.

Chilled cucumber soup

Nothing beats a chilled cucumber soup on a hot, balmy day: it cools the body and whets the appetite. I find a little horseradish cream brings the soup alive, but you can leave it out to keep the flavours subtle and light.

Peel the cucumbers and cut 2 lengthways into quarters. Slice off the seedy core from each quarter, then chop into dice. Put into a large bowl and set aside.

Peel the remaining cucumber into long thin ribbons using a swivel vegetable peeler. (Cut the ribbons in half if you find them too long.) Place in another bowl and toss with a little lemon juice, the olive oil, chopped dill, and salt and pepper. Cover with cling film and chill until ready to serve.

Put half the yoghurt, a pinch of salt and pepper and half the chopped cucumber into a blender. Whiz to a smooth purée. Press the purée through a fine sieve, pushing down hard with the back of a ladle. Discard the cucumber pulp in the sieve. Repeat the process with the remaining chopped cucumber and yoghurt. Taste and adjust the seasoning of the cucumber purée, adding 1 or 2 tablespoons of horseradish cream or a squeeze of lemon juice, as desired. Cover with cling film and chill if not serving immediately.

To serve, pour the cold soup into chilled bowls and garnish with the dressed cucumber ribbons and dill fronds.

SERVES 4

3 long cucumbers, about 650g each, straight from the refrigerator
lemon juice, to taste
1 tbsp olive oil
handful of dill, leaves roughly chopped, plus few fronds to garnish
500ml natural yoghurt
1–2 tbsp horseradish cream, or to taste

Curried cauliflower and cheddar soup

A little curry powder and saffron elevate the classic combination of cauliflower and cheese to another dimension in this soup. It is ideal as a winter warmer, as well as a comforting and welcoming treat for Bonfire Night. Delicious served with warm Indian bread or cheddar on toast.

SERVES 6 AS A STARTER OR 4 AS A LIGHT LUNCH
4 tbsp olive oil
2 medium onions, chopped
2 celery stalks, chopped
1 medium head of cauliflower, cut into florets
1 tsp mild curry powder
pinch of saffron strands
300ml hot chicken or vegetable stock (see pages 258–9)
300ml milk
100g medium or strong cheddar, grated

Heat half the oil in a large saucepan and add the onions and celery. Stir over medium heat for 3–4 minutes until the vegetables are beginning to soften. Add the remaining oil, cauliflower florets, curry powder and saffron, and season with salt and pepper. Stir well and cook for a couple of minutes. Cover the pan and cook for another 4–5 minutes, lifting the lid to give the mixture a stir every now and then.

Remove the lid and pour in the chicken stock. Bring to a simmer, then pour in the milk, adding a splash of water if the liquid does not cover the vegetables. Return to a gentle simmer. Partially cover the pan and simmer for 10 minutes until the cauliflower is very soft.

Use a hand-held stick blender to liquidize the soup, or blend the soup in 2 batches if using a regular blender. Return the soup to the pan and place over low heat. Bring to a gentle simmer, then slowly stir in the cheese to melt. Loosen the consistency with a little hot water if the soup is too thick, and taste and adjust the seasoning.

Roast chestnut, parsnip and apple soup

The subtle nutty flavour of chestnuts is paired with sweet apples and parsnips in this creamy soup. I love this earthy combination of flavours, and the soup makes for an easy lunch when served with cheddar on toast. Save time by using a packet of vacuum-packed chestnuts, or at Christmas, use up any leftover roasted chestnuts.

Melt the butter in a wide pan and add the parsnips, celery and a little seasoning. Stir over high heat for 4–6 minutes until the vegetables are lightly golden. Tip in the apples and cook, stirring occasionally, for another 4–5 minutes until the apples are soft.

Add the chestnuts, pour in the stock to cover and bring to a simmer. Cook for another 5–10 minutes, then remove the pan from the heat. Use a hand-held stick blender or a regular blender to liquidize the soup to a smooth and creamy purée.

Return the soup to the pan, and taste and adjust the seasoning. If you prefer the soup thinner, loosen the consistency with a splash of boiling water. Reheat gently just before serving. Serve in warm bowls with swirls of cream.

SERVES 4 AS A STARTER
20g butter
2 medium parsnips, chopped
2 celery stalks, chopped
2 apples, peeled, cored and chopped
250g roasted chestnuts, shelled, skinned and roughly chopped
600ml hot chicken or vegetable stock (see pages 258–9)
few tbsp single cream, to serve

Asparagus velouté

The delicate flavour of asparagus comes through in this smooth and velvety soup. At the restaurant, we would use asparagus trimmings to make the velouté, reserving all the young, tender spears for salads and for garnishes. You could do the same, using a mixture of older stalks and any peelings you have. The soup can be served hot or well chilled.

SERVES 4 AS A STARTER

2 large bunches of asparagus (about 800g)
1½ tbsp olive oil, plus extra to drizzle
30g butter
1 medium onion, chopped
1 celery stalk, chopped

stripped leaves from a sprig of thyme
about 700ml hot chicken or vegetable stock
(see pages 258–9)
squeeze of lemon juice (optional)
150ml double cream

Pick out 12 of the most attractive asparagus spears and cut off the tips to use for garnish. Roughly chop the rest and set aside.

Heat the oil and half the butter in a large pan. Add the onion, celery and some seasoning and cook for 4–6 minutes, stirring frequently, until the vegetables begin to soften. Add the chopped asparagus and thyme, and stir over high heat for another 3–4 minutes until the asparagus is tender but still vibrant green. Pour in just enough stock to cover, and simmer for 2 minutes. Remove the pan from the heat.

Blend the soup in 2 batches while it is still hot: place half the vegetables in a blender using a slotted spoon, add 1 or 2 ladles of hot stock and blend well. Push the resulting purée through a fine sieve, pressing down hard with the back of a ladle. Discard the pulp and repeat with the remaining soup. Gradually add more hot stock to the strained purée until you get a creamy consistency. Taste and adjust the seasoning, adding a little lemon juice if you like, and erring towards the side of over-seasoning if you intend to serve the soup cold.

When ready to serve, add the cream and gently reheat until it just comes to a simmer. Meanwhile, sauté the asparagus tips with the remaining butter and some seasoning in a hot frying pan. Add a splash of water and cover the pan. Let the asparagus steam for 2–3 minutes until just tender.

Pour the soup into warm bowls and garnish with the asparagus tips. Drizzle over a little olive oil and serve immediately.

Alnwick soup

I've used the core ingredients of the classic Alnwick stew to make this hearty soup. The broth is light and flavourful, and at the same time, the chunks of ham and vegetables are nourishing and satisfying. Eat with rye or seeded bread. Comfort in a bowl.

Cut off the rind and excess fat from the ham hocks, then place in a large pot. Cover with cold water and bring to the boil. Reduce the heat and leave to simmer for 10 minutes. Pour off the water and the scum on top.

Add the onion, carrot, celery, bay leaf, thyme and peppercorns to the pot to join the ham hocks. Cover with fresh water and bring to a simmer. Gently cook for about 2½–3 hours until the meat is tender and falling off the bone. Turn the hocks around halfway through to ensure even cooking. When ready, leave the hocks to cool in the liquid.

Remove the ham hocks to a large bowl with a pair of tongs. Pull the meat off the bone and tear into bite-size chunks. Strain the stock into a clean saucepan and discard the vegetables, herbs and peppercorns. Add the onions, potatoes, celery and thyme to the strained stock and bring to a simmer. Cook for 30–40 minutes until the vegetables are soft. Add the ham pieces and simmer for another 10 minutes to warm through. Ladle into warm soup bowls and sprinkle with parsley to serve.

SERVES 4–6
Broth:
2 smoked ham hocks, about 750g
1 large onion, roughly chopped
2 large carrots, roughly chopped
2 celery stalks, roughly chopped
1 bay leaf
few sprigs of thyme
½ tsp black peppercorns

To finish:
2 large onions, roughly chopped
2 large waxy potatoes, cut into bite-size chunks
2 celery stalks, roughly chopped
few sprigs of thyme
generous handful of flat-leaf parsley, leaves chopped

Broccoli, stilton and pear soup

A soup that's the perfect starter for entertaining, both for its elegance and its ease of preparation. The broccoli soup can be prepared a day in advance, ready to reheat just before serving. It is best to peel and roast the pears to serve, but if you decide to prepare them earlier, put them in water with a squeeze of lemon juice to prevent them from turning brown, then drain and pat dry with kitchen paper before roasting so they caramelize nicely.

SERVES 4
2 large heads of broccoli, about 1kg
800ml hot chicken or vegetable stock (see pages 258–9)
100g stilton, crumbled
2 firm but ripe pears
25g butter
handful of toasted flaked almonds, to garnish

Cut the broccoli into florets, but do not waste the stalks. Peel off the tough skins from the stalks and roughly chop up the tender core.

Bring the stock to the boil in a medium saucepan. Add the broccoli and cover the pan. Cook for 3–4 minutes until the broccoli is tender but still bright green. In 2 batches, blend the broccoli into a smooth soup, adding half the stilton as you do so. Return the soup to the pan. Taste and adjust the seasoning and reheat just before serving.

Peel the pears and cut them in half lengthways. Remove the cores with an apple corer. Melt the butter in a pan and add the pear halves, cut-side down. Spoon over the foaming butter to baste as you cook the pears. Pan-roast them on one side for 1–2 minutes until they are golden brown around the edges, then flip them over to roast the other side. Cook for another 1–2 minutes, then remove to a plate and drain off the excess butter.

Pour the soup into warm bowls and rest a pan-roasted pear half in the centre. Scatter over the remaining crumbled stilton and the flaked almonds. Serve at once.

Conger eel bisque

Conger eels are considered a delicacy by the French and Japanese, and rightly so. Here I've used the eel as a base for a flavourful fish soup. It's rich, so serve it in small bowls as a starter with a few garlic croutes on the side.

SERVES 4–6
2kg conger eel fillets (get your fishmonger to remove the skin and cut the meat into boneless fillets)
pinch of saffron strands
olive oil, for cooking
1 fennel bulb, finely sliced
1 carrot, chopped
2 celery stalks, chopped
1 shallot, chopped
2 garlic cloves, crushed
2 star anise
generous pinch of cayenne pepper
250ml Pernod or Noilly Prat
1 large potato, about 300g, finely diced
5 vine-ripened plum tomatoes, deseeded and chopped
sprig each of basil and flat-leaf parsley, leaves chopped
1 litre hot fish stock (see page 262)
squeeze of lemon juice (optional)

Season the eel fillets with salt, pepper and saffron, then drizzle over a little olive oil. Toss well to coat evenly. Heat a thin layer of olive oil in a wide pan. Fry the eel fillets in batches over a moderate heat for 2–3 minutes on each side. Remove to a plate and set aside.

Add a little more oil to the pan and toss in the fennel, carrot, celery, shallot, garlic, star anise and cayenne pepper. Stir frequently over a medium heat for a few minutes. Pour in the Pernod and boil until reduced to a syrupy consistency. Add the potato, tomatoes and herbs, then return the eel to the pan. Pour in enough stock to cover and bring to a simmer. Cook gently for about 15–20 minutes until the potatoes are very soft.

Fish out and discard the star anise. In batches, blend the soup until smooth, holding a tea towel over the blender as you blitz to avoid hot-soup splatters. Strain the soup through a fine sieve into a clean pan, pressing down to extract all the liquid.

Return the soup to a gentle simmer and reheat for a few minutes. Taste and adjust the seasoning, adding a squeeze of lemon juice if you wish. Pour into warm soup bowls and serve immediately.

Italian-style turnip soup

This is a great quick and healthy soup for a weeknight supper. It is also ideal for vegetarians – simply omit the bacon and use vegetable stock. You also could add a mixture of root vegetables and replace the rice with macaroni or other pasta.

Heat the butter and oil in a large saucepan. As the butter begins to foam, add the bacon and fry for 3–4 minutes until golden brown. Stir in the onion, turnips and some salt and pepper and cook for another 6–8 minutes until the vegetables are soft and lightly golden. Tip in the rice and stir well, adding a little more oil if necessary. Toast the rice for a minute, then pour in the stock to cover. Give the mixture a stir, then partially cover the pan. Simmer gently for 15–20 minutes until the rice is tender. Taste and adjust the seasoning, and add a little boiling water as necessary to increase the broth.

Just before serving, stir in 2 tbsp of parmesan. Ladle the soup into warm bowls and sprinkle over the remaining parmesan and the chopped parsley. Serve immediately.

SERVES 4–6

knob of butter
1 tbsp olive oil, plus extra to drizzle
3 rashers of streaky bacon, chopped
1 medium onion, chopped into 1cm dice
450g turnips, chopped into 1cm dice
150g risotto rice, such as carnaroli, vialone nano or arborio
800ml hot chicken or vegetable stock (see pages 258–9)
5–6 heaped tbsp freshly grated parmesan
handful of flat-leaf parsley, leaves chopped

Cornish crab soup

This crab soup instantly transports me to lovely holidays by the Cornish coast. It may seem like a lot of effort to pick out the flesh from the crab and use the shells to make your own stock, but, trust me, the results are well worth it.

SERVES 4

1 large cooked crab, about 1.5kg
3 tbsp olive oil
1 onion, finely chopped
1 large carrot, finely chopped
2 celery stalks, finely chopped
1 large garlic clove, sliced
1 lemongrass stalk, roughly chopped

1 tbsp tomato purée
splash of brandy or cognac
200ml Noilly Prat or dry white wine
3 plum tomatoes, chopped
sprig each of basil, tarragon and parsley
3–4 tbsp crème fraiche
handful of coriander leaves, to garnish

Remove the flesh from the crab shell: twist off the legs and claws from the body. Turn over the body so the pale belly is facing upwards. Pull the belly shell to remove it in a single piece. Discard along with the small sac and furry grey gills (known as dead man's fingers). Use a small spoon to scrape out the brown and white meat from the body, keeping them in separate bowls. Crack open the claws and legs and extract the flesh with a skewer or a crab pick.

Use the back of a Chinese cleaver, a strong chef's knife or a pestle to break up the crab shell into small pieces. Place them in a large bowl.

Now make the crab stock: heat the oil in a large pot and add the onion, carrot, celery, garlic and lemongrass. Stir over high heat for 4–6 minutes until the vegetables are golden and beginning to soften. Add the crab shells, tomato purée and a splash of brandy or cognac and stir well. Fry for another 4–5 minutes, stirring frequently. Add the Noilly Prat and boil for a few minutes until reduced by two-thirds. Pour in enough water to cover, about 750–800ml, and bring to a simmer. Skim off any scum or froth from the surface of the liquid, then add the tomatoes and herbs. Simmer for 20 minutes.

Strain the stock through a fine sieve into a clean pan. Discard the shells and vegetables. Bring the stock to the boil and let it bubble vigorously until reduced by a third, to about 500ml. Stir in a few tablespoons of crème fraiche and season well to taste.

Spoon the brown and white crabmeat into the centre of warmed bowls and pour the piping hot soup around. (You could also add the crabmeat to the gently simmering soup to warm through before serving.) Garnish with coriander leaves and serve.

Oxtail soup

Oxtail is still a relatively cheap cut, and the gelatinous nature of the meat makes it ideal for soups and stews. I remember it as one of my favourite soups when I was growing up, and I think it's a shame this warming and delicious soup isn't as popular as it used to be.

SERVES 4

1 oxtail, about 1.5kg, jointed
4 tbsp plain flour
2–3 tbsp olive oil
1 large carrot, roughly chopped
1 turnip, roughly chopped
1 celery stalk, roughly chopped
1 large onion, roughly chopped

1 bay leaf
few sprigs of thyme
1 tsp black peppercorns
2 tsp tomato purée
300ml red wine
1.2 litres hot beef stock (see page 259)
2 tbsp butter, softened
handful of flat-leaf parsley, leaves chopped

Trim off any excess fat from the oxtail pieces. In a shallow bowl, mix 2 tablespoons of the flour with some salt and pepper. Heat half the oil in a large heavy-based or cast-iron pan until hot. Coat the oxtail pieces with the seasoned flour, shaking off any excess, and fry for 2–2½ minutes on each side until evenly browned all over. Remove the oxtail to a plate and set aside.

Add the remaining oil to the pan along with the chopped vegetables, herbs and peppercorns. Cook for 4–5 minutes until the vegetables begin to soften. Stir in the tomato purée and remaining seasoned flour, adding a little more oil as necessary. Stir frequently for another minute or 2.

Pour in the red wine and scrape the base of the pan with a wooden spoon to dislodge the sediment. Boil for a few minutes. Return the oxtail to the pan and pour in the stock to cover. Bring to a simmer and skim off any scum that rises to the surface. Partially cover the pan and cook gently for 3 hours until the oxtail is very tender and comes off the bone easily. With a pair of kitchen tongs, lift out the oxtail pieces to a large bowl and leave to cool slightly.

Strain the cooking stock through a fine sieve into a clean pan, pushing down on the vegetables with the back of a ladle to extract as much liquid as possible. Pull the meat from the oxtail and shred into small pieces. To thicken the stock, mix the remaining 2 tablespoons of flour with the butter, then whisk into the simmering stock, a little at a time. Simmer for 5 minutes. Taste and adjust the seasoning of the soup, then add the shredded meat to the pan to warm through. Sprinkle with lots of chopped parsley before serving.

Shropshire summer soup

Shropshire summer soups are traditionally served smooth and creamy. I prefer mine rustic – chunky vegetables in a light broth. If you decide to liquidize the soup, mix in some double cream after blending for richness and to give it a silky texture.

Heat a large pan with the oil and add the onions and potatoes. Stir frequently over medium heat for 4–5 minutes. Meanwhile, peel, core and chop the marrow into 1cm dice. Add the marrow, thyme leaves and some salt and pepper and cook for another couple of minutes.

Pour in the stock and bring to the boil. Lower the heat and simmer for 5 minutes. Taste and adjust the seasoning. Add the little gem lettuce and turn off the heat as soon as the lettuce has wilted. Scatter over half the chopped herbs. Ladle the hot soup into warm bowls and garnish with the remaining chopped herbs to serve.

SERVES 4–6

4 tbsp olive oil

2 medium onions, chopped into 1cm dice

2 large potatoes, about 450g, chopped into 1cm dice

half a marrow, about 500g

stripped leaves from a few sprigs of thyme

1 litre hot vegetable or chicken stock (see pages 258–9)

2 heads of little gem lettuce, finely shredded

handful each of flat-leaf parsley and mint, leaves chopped

Crayfish chowder

Our rivers are teeming with crayfish. More of us should consider cooking them! Not only are they plentiful and cheap, they are delicious in salads, in rice and pasta dishes, and especially in soups, such as this New England-style chowder. This dish is quite substantial. With sourdough bread and a light salad, it makes a good lunch.

SERVES 4

Crayfish stock:
1.5–2kg live crayfish
2 tbsp olive oil
1 onion, chopped
1 carrot, chopped
1 celery stalk, chopped
2 bay leaves
few sprigs of thyme
2 tbsp tomato purée
200ml dry white wine
1 plum tomato, chopped

Chowder:
25g butter
1 leek, finely chopped
1 carrot, finely chopped
20g plain flour
1 potato, finely diced
150g sweetcorn kernels, thawed if frozen
squeeze of lemon juice, to taste
4 tbsp crème fraiche, to serve (optional)
handful of flat-leaf parsley, leaves chopped

Bring a stockpot of water to the boil. Cook the crayfish in 2 batches: add half to the pan and return to the boil. Cook for 3 minutes, then remove with a pair of tongs and refresh in a large bowl of iced water. Repeat with the remaining crayfish.

Drain the crayfish and remove the meat. First, pull out the claws. Snip the shell underneath the tail with kitchen scissors, take out the tail flesh and set aside. If you have the time and patience, crack the claws and extract the small pieces of flesh from there, too. Set aside with the flesh from the tails. Place the heads and shells in a large bowl and bash them with a pestle or the end of a rolling pin to break them into smaller pieces.

Heat the oil in a large stockpot. Stir in the onion, carrot, celery and herbs. Cook for 4–6 minutes over high heat until the vegetables are lightly browned. Add the tomato purée and crayfish shells. Stir over high heat for 4–5 minutes.

Pour in the white wine and boil until it has almost all reduced and the pan is quite dry. Add the chopped tomato and pour in enough water to cover the shells. Bring to a simmer and cook gently for 15–20 minutes. When ready, strain the stock through a fine sieve into a clean pot and discard the shells and vegetables. Boil the stock until reduced to about 800ml.

For the chowder, melt the butter in a large pot and stir in the leek, carrot and a little salt and pepper. Sauté over medium heat for 4–6 minutes until the vegetables begin to soften. Add the flour and stir frequently for another couple of minutes. Pour in the crayfish stock and tip in the potatoes. Simmer for 5 minutes until the potatoes are tender. Add the sweetcorn and cook for 2–3 minutes until tender.

Adjust the seasoning, adding a little lemon juice to taste. Add the crayfish flesh to the soup and heat for a few minutes to warm through. Ladle into warm bowls and serve immediately with a dollop of crème fraiche and a sprinkling of chopped parsley.

Jacket potato soup with sour cream

This soup was inspired by one I had many years ago at the acclaimed *El Bulli* restaurant in Spain. The clear broth is infused with the flavour of baked potatoes and served with home-made potato gnocchi: a surprising and delightful mouthful of flavours and textures.

SERVES 4–6 AS A STARTER

4 large baking potatoes,
   about 750g
800ml clear chicken or vegetable stock
   (see pages 258–9)
150ml sour cream
handful of chives, finely chopped

Gnocchi:
150g plain flour
1 tsp fine sea salt
2½ tbsp grated parmesan
2 tbsp olive oil, plus extra to drizzle
1 medium egg, lightly beaten

Preheat the oven to 180°C/Gas 4. Wash the potatoes well, pat dry with kitchen paper and wrap in large sheet of foil. Bake for 1½ hours until tender when pierced with a skewer. Remove from the oven and turn down the setting to 150°C/Gas 2. Wearing rubber gloves to protect your hands, peel the skins off the potatoes while still hot. Spread the skins out on a baking tray and bake for 15–20 minutes until dry and crisp. Turn off the oven, but leave the skins inside to dry out further.

Meanwhile, make the gnocchi. Mash the potatoes using a potato ricer. Leave to cool completely. Measure out 400g (save the rest for another dish). Mix in the flour, salt and parmesan. Add the olive oil and slowly incorporate the egg until the mixture comes together to form a dough; you may not need all the egg. Lightly knead the dough on a floured surface until smooth. Divide into four balls. Roll out each ball into a long, skinny sausage about 1–2cm thick. Cut the dough into 1cm pieces, then roll lightly between your palms to neaten the shape, but you don't need to make perfect rounds.

Bring a pot of salted water to the boil and have ready a bowl of iced water. Blanch the gnocchi in batches for 2–3 minutes or until they float to the surface. Remove with a slotted spoon and immediately plunge into the iced water. Drain well and toss in a bowl with a generous drizzle of olive oil and some seasoning.

For the soup, bring the stock to the boil in a pan with a pinch of salt and pepper. Tip in the crispy potato skins and reduce the heat to a low simmer. Cover the pan and gently simmer for 30–40 minutes until the skins have imparted their colour and flavour to the stock. Strain through a fine sieve into a clean pan. Discard the skins. When ready to serve, reheat the gnocchi in the potato-infused broth and simmer for a minute. Divide among warm bowls and garnish with spoonfuls of sour cream and chopped chives.

Creamy sorrel soup

There is no match for the distinctive zesty and peppery flavour of sorrel. I cook with it as much as possible when it is in season. This soup is one of my favourites, and is equally delicious hot or cold. Make sure the stock is piping hot when you add the sorrel to the pan so that the leaves wilt quickly and you retain their vibrant green colour.

SERVES 4
2 large bunches of sorrel, about 150–175g, washed
3 tbsp olive oil
1 large Spanish onion, chopped
1 large potato, about 300g, finely diced
800ml hot chicken or vegetable stock (see pages 258–9)
150ml sour cream
handful of red-vein sorrel leaves, to garnish (optional)

Roughly chop the sorrel and set aside. Heat the oil in a saucepan and add the onion, potato and some seasoning. Stir well and cover the pan with a lid. Cook over medium-to-low heat for 10 minutes, lifting the lid every once in a while to give the mixture a stir. When the potato is soft, pour in the hot stock and boil for a few minutes. Tip in the sorrel, and as soon as the leaves begin to wilt, immediately remove the pan from the heat. In 2 batches, transfer the soup into a blender and blitz until very smooth. Hold a tea towel over the lid of the blender to avoid burning your hands with the hot soup, should it splash out.

Stir in half of the sour cream and reheat the soup if necessary. Pour into warm bowls and garnish with a spoonful of sour cream and, if you wish, some red-vein sorrel.

pasta
and grains

At home, we don't just stick to rice and spaghetti. Tana has begun to feed the kids a vegetarian meal once a week, which means being creative in combining pulses, grains and pasta with a variety of vegetables. The kids love it when she experiments. When the weather is cold we use a lot of barley, adding it to soups, stews and winter salads. Barley can even take the place of rice in a risotto. The excellent barley risotto here has featured many a time on our restaurant menus.

My love affair with pasta stems from the time I spent in Sicily and Sardinia as a young chef. When I finally returned to London and opened *Aubergine* back in October 1993, I was determined to include handmade pasta on the menu. Fresh pasta can be mind-blowing, and any young chef joining our brigade had to master the art of making it. It is a fundamental skill in our kitchens.

Farfalle with bacon, peas and sage
Fresh tagliatelle with stilton and mushrooms
Grilled vegetable lasagne
Conchiglie with meaty tomato ragù
Penne with baked pumpkin and rosemary
Spaghetti with broccoli, garlic and chilli
Chorizo, broad bean and mint couscous
Linguine with lemon, feta and basil
Smoked haddock with white beans and parsley
Gordon's posh kedgeree
Spinach, mushroom and ricotta cannelloni
Goat's cheese, beetroot and lentil salad
Wild mushroom barley risotto
Herby rice pilaf with pistachios and almonds

Farfalle with bacon, peas and sage

This is an easy pasta carbonara, without any egg yolks, so there is no chance of splitting the sauce. My kids must have this for tea once a week – they love it! (Illustrated on page 50.)

SERVES 4
400g dried farfalle
3 tbsp olive oil
150g bacon lardons or 8 rashers of streaky bacon, chopped
1 large garlic clove, finely chopped
300ml double cream
150g peas, thawed if frozen
60g freshly grated parmesan, plus extra to sprinkle
small handful each of sage and flat-leaf parsley, leaves only

Bring a pot of salted water to the boil. Tip in the farfalle and cook according to packet instructions until the pasta is al dente.

Heat the oil in another pan and add the bacon. Fry over high heat for 3–4 minutes until the bacon is golden brown. Add the garlic and fry for a minute. Pour in the cream and bring to the boil. Let simmer for 5 minutes until reduced and thickened slightly. Tip in the peas, bring back to a simmer and cook for another 3–4 minutes. Stir the grated parmesan into the sauce, then taste and adjust the seasoning.

When the pasta is ready, drain it in a colander and immediately tip into the sauce. Add the herbs, then toss the pasta until well coated with the creamy sauce. Divide among warm plates and sprinkle over a little more parmesan to serve.

Fresh tagliatelle with stilton and mushrooms

Tana likes to make this towards year end, using leftover stilton from Christmas. Of course, you can use any blue cheese: piquant roquefort, savoury dolcelatte or creamy gorgonzola would work well.

Bring a large pot of salted water to the boil. In the meantime, melt the butter in a wide sauté pan. When it begins to foam, add the mushrooms and some seasoning. Fry over high heat, tossing occasionally, until the mushrooms are golden brown and tender. Add the cream and reduce the heat.

Cook the tagliatelle in the boiling water for 2 minutes until al dente. Drain the pasta, but reserve 4–5 tablespoons of the water in the pan. Return the tagliatelle to the pan and tip in the mushrooms and cream. Add three-quarters of the stilton and half of the chopped herbs and toss until the pasta is evenly coated with the melting cheese and sauce.

Divide among individual serving plates and scatter over the remaining stilton and herbs. Serve at once.

SERVES 6
25g butter
250g chestnut or baby portabella mushrooms, sliced
100ml double cream
500g fresh tagliatelle
100g stilton, chopped or crumbled
handful each of fresh oregano and flat-leaf parsley, leaves chopped

Grilled vegetable lasagne

Food like this is far too good to leave to the vegetarians. If you have time, make the tomato sauce the day before to let the flavours balance out.

SERVES 4–6
300g fresh lasagne sheets (about 12)
75g freshly grated parmesan
3 x 150g buffalo mozzarella, thinly sliced
leaves from a small handful of basil

Grilled vegetables:
1 small aubergine
1 large green courgette
1 large yellow courgette
1 yellow pepper
1 red pepper
olive oil, to drizzle
few sprigs of thyme and rosemary

Tomato and basil sauce:
2 tbsp olive oil
1 onion, chopped
2 celery stalks, chopped
1 carrot, finely diced
2 garlic cloves, finely chopped
stripped leaves from a sprig of thyme
2 x 400g tins chopped tomatoes in
   natural juice
1 tsp caster sugar (optional)
small handful of basil, leaves torn

First, make the tomato sauce. Heat the oil in a saucepan over medium heat. Add the onion, celery, carrot, garlic and thyme with some salt and pepper. Stir frequently and cook for about 6–8 minutes until the vegetables are soft. Tip in the tomatoes and bring to a simmer. Simmer gently for 30 minutes, stirring occasionally, until the sauce has reduced and thickened slightly. Taste and add sugar if the tomatoes seem acidic.

Meanwhile, prepare the vegetables. Trim the aubergine and courgettes, then slice into 5mm rounds. Drizzle with olive oil and season. Cook in batches on a hot griddle pan for 2–3 minutes on each side until tender and lightly charred. Transfer to a large bowl.

Preheat the grill to hot. Cut the red and yellow peppers in half and place them cut-side down on a lightly oiled baking sheet. Grill for 10–15 minutes until well charred. Remove and leave to cool slightly before peeling off the skins and discarding the seeds. Cut the flesh into wedges and add to the bowl of grilled vegetables.

When the tomato sauce is ready, add the basil, transfer to a food processor and blitz until smooth. Taste and adjust the seasoning. Tip into a bowl and leave to cool.

Preheat the oven to 180°C/Gas 4. Spoon a thin layer of tomato sauce over the base of a deep baking dish. Put two sheets of lasagne on top, then sprinkle over a little parmesan. Arrange a layer of grilled vegetables on top, followed by a layer of mozzarella and a layer of tomato sauce. Repeat until you've reached the top of the dish. You want to finish with a layer of lasagne sheets spread generously with tomato sauce. Top this with a final layer of mozzarella cheese and a sprinkling of parmesan. Bake for 30–40 minutes until the cheese topping is golden brown and the sauce is bubbling around the sides.

Conchiglie with meaty tomato ragù

This is my version of a pasta bolognese. I prefer to use conchiglie, as their shell shape holds more of the flavourful sauce than spaghetti does. Meat ragù freezes well and makes an ideal prepare-ahead supper.

SERVES 4

Ragù:
3 tbsp olive oil
1 large onion, finely chopped
2 garlic cloves, finely chopped
1 celery stalk, finely chopped
1 carrot, finely chopped
stripped leaves from a sprig of thyme
1 tbsp chopped rosemary
500g lean beef mince
150ml dry white wine

400g tin chopped tomatoes in juice
300ml chicken stock (see page 258) or water
pinch of caster sugar (optional)

Pasta:
400g dried conchiglie
large handful of flat-leaf parsley and
  oregano, chopped
parmesan, to serve

Heat a tablespoon of olive oil in a large heavy-based pan until hot. Add the onion and some seasoning. Fry over medium heat, stirring frequently, for 6–8 minutes until the onion begins to soften. Tip in the garlic, celery, carrot and herbs. Sauté briefly over high heat for a few minutes, until the vegetables are lightly golden.

Add the remaining oil and the beef mince. Stir well, pressing down on the mince to break it up. Season again and continue to stir over high heat until the mince is no longer red. Pour in the wine and let it boil vigorously until almost all reduced and the pan is quite dry.

Reduce the heat to medium and add the tomatoes and stock. Stir well to mix. When the liquid in the pan begins to boil, turn the heat to the lowest setting and partially cover the pan. Cook gently for 2½–3 hours, stirring occasionally. Taste and adjust the seasoning, adding a pinch of sugar, if necessary, to balance the acidity of the tomatoes.

Fifteen minutes before you are ready to serve, bring a large pan of salted water to the boil. Cook the pasta according to packet instructions until al dente. As soon as the pasta is ready, drain it off and immediately add to the hot ragù, stirring in the chopped herbs as well. Divide among warm plates and serve with a generous grating of black pepper and parmesan.

Penne with baked pumpkin and rosemary

There are two ways to serve this: with a smooth or a chunky sauce. It depends both on your taste and on the firmness of the pumpkin flesh. If you can get them, baby bear and small sugar pumpkins have firm orange flesh and a sweetness that will caramelize well on cooking.

Heat the oven to 200°C/Gas 6. Cut the pumpkin into thin wedges. Spread a little olive oil over the base of a roasting tray and sprinkle over a little salt and pepper. Arrange the pumpkin in a single layer and drizzle generously with more olive oil. Scatter over the garlic, herbs and a little more seasoning. Bake for 20–25 minutes until the pumpkin is soft. Remove from the oven and leave to cool for a few minutes. Meanwhile, bring a pot of salted water to the boil.

Reserving the oil in the roasting tray (discard the herbs and garlic pulp; they have done their job), remove the skin from the pumpkin and cut the flesh into small bite-size chunks. If making a smooth sauce, put the pumpkin along with the reserved oil into a food processor and blend to a smooth purée. Transfer to a small saucepan. Bring to the boil and let it bubble until reduced to a consistency that will coat the pasta well.

Cook the penne according to packet instructions until al dente. Drain into a colander and return to the hot pan. Add the pumpkin purée and grated parmesan and toss well. If you've decided to leave the pumpkins in chunks, simply toss them and the reserved oil with the pasta and parmesan. Taste and adjust the seasoning. Divide among individual plates and sprinkle each plate with a small handful of parmesan shavings to serve.

SERVES 4–6 AS A STARTER OR LIGHT LUNCH
500g wedge of cooking pumpkin, skin on
olive oil, to drizzle
4 garlic cloves, halved with skin on
leaves from a few sprigs of rosemary
few sprigs of thyme
400g dried penne
30g freshly grated parmesan, plus shavings to serve

Spaghetti with broccoli, garlic and chilli

I first tasted this pasta dish in Sicily, and it blew me away. Who would have thought a little garlic, chilli and broccoli could make a delicious spaghetti sauce? The key is to flavour good-quality olive oil with the garlic and chilli over low-ish heat before you add the broccoli. You don't want the garlic to colour too much or it will overpower the dish.

SERVES 4
400g dried spaghetti
4 tbsp olive oil
5 large garlic cloves, finely sliced
1 red chilli, deseeded and finely chopped
1 large head of broccoli, cut into small florets
splash of water or chicken stock (see page 258)
squeeze of lemon juice, to taste
extra virgin olive oil, to drizzle

Bring a large pot of salted water to the boil. Add the spaghetti and cook according to packet instructions until al dente.

A few minutes before the pasta is ready, heat a large sauté pan with the oil over low-to-medium heat. Add the garlic, chilli and a pinch of salt and sauté for a minute. When the garlic becomes sticky and very lightly golden around the edges, add the broccoli and a splash of water. Cover the pan with a lid and leave to steam for 2 minutes. Remove the lid, squeeze over the lemon juice and toss the broccoli with a little more seasoning.

Drain the pasta and immediately tip into the sauté pan, adding a little of the salted water from the pan to help create a sauce. Drizzle over a little extra virgin olive oil and check the seasoning. Divide among warm plates and serve at once.

Chorizo, broad bean and mint couscous

This makes a fantastic accompaniment to the red mullet with anchovy sauce (see page 96) or you can double the recipe to serve it on its own.

First, put the kettle on to boil. Place the couscous and a generous pinch of salt and pepper in a large heatproof bowl and stir to mix. As soon as the water has boiled, measure out 300ml and pour over the couscous. Cover the bowl with a piece of cling film and leave to stand for 10–15 minutes.

Heat the oil in a frying pan and add the shallots and ground spices. Stir frequently for 6–8 minutes until the shallots are soft. Add the chorizo and fry for another 3–4 minutes until cooked through. Stir in the broad beans and cook for another 1–2 minutes until warmed through. Remove the pan from the heat.

Unwrap the cling film and fork the couscous to fluff up the grains. Add the contents of the frying pan to the couscous and mix well. Taste and adjust the seasoning. Finally, stir through the chopped mint and serve warm.

SERVES 4 AS A SIDE DISH
250g couscous
75ml olive oil
2 large shallots, finely chopped
½ tsp ground cumin
½ tsp ground coriander
pinch of paprika
200g fresh chorizo sausage, skin removed and chopped
200g blanched and skinned broad beans
large handful of mint, leaves chopped

Linguine with lemon, feta and basil

The light and zesty flavour of this pasta makes it ideal for the summer. It's also a quick and easy supper dish, as you are likely to have the ingredients to hand.

SERVES 4
500g fresh (or 300g dried) linguine
4 tbsp olive oil
juice and zest of 1 lemon
5 tbsp freshly grated parmesan
leaves from a handful of basil
200g feta cheese, crumbled
2 tbsp toasted pine nuts

Cook the fresh pasta in a large pot of salted boiling water for 2 minutes. If using dried pasta, cook according to pack instructions until al dente. Tip the pasta into a colander and drain off most of the water, leaving about 2 tablespoons in the pan. Immediately return the pasta to the pan and add the olive oil, lemon juice and zest, parmesan, basil and three-quarters of the crumbled feta. Toss well and check the seasoning. Divide among warm plates and scatter over the remaining feta and pine nuts. Serve at once.

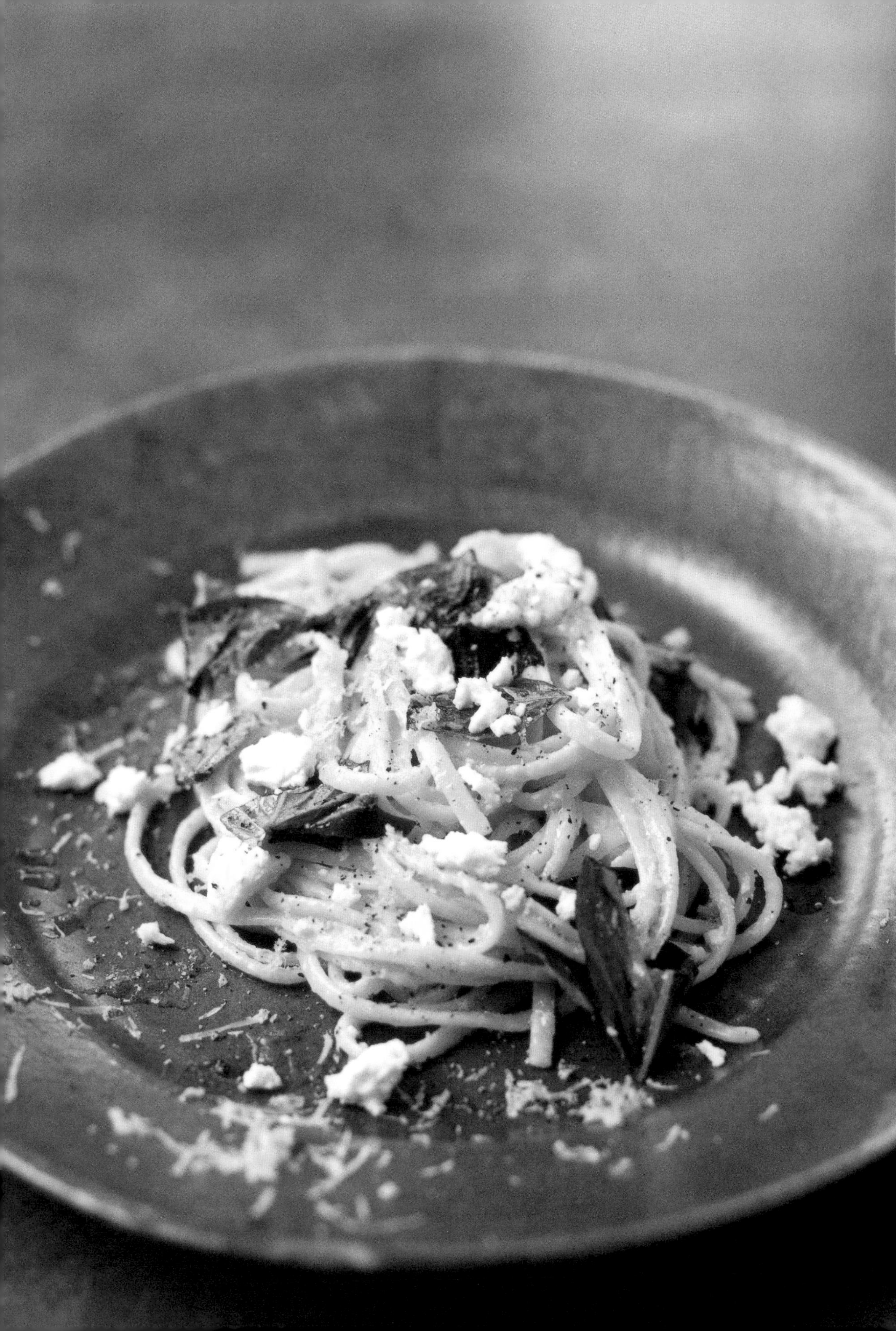

Smoked haddock with white beans and parsley

A little smoked bacon enhances the flavour of smoked haddock in this surf-and-turf combination. Use good-quality, undyed, lightly smoked haddock to get the most from the dish.

Put the beans, bacon, thyme and garlic in a pan and fill with water to cover. Boil for 1–1¼ hours until the beans are soft. Use a slotted spoon to transfer half the beans to a blender. Add a ladleful or two of the cooking liquid and liquidize to a fine purée. Transfer the purée to a clean saucepan. Drain off the remaining beans, reserving the cooking liquid, and add to the pan. Remove and discard the bacon, thyme and garlic. Stir well, adding a little more cooking liquid if the mixture is too thick. Keep warm.

For the smoked haddock, fry the bacon with half the oil until crisp. Heat another frying pan with the remaining oil until hot. Add the haddock fillets to the pan and fry for a minute. Add a few knobs of butter to melt, and throw in the thyme sprigs and parsley leaves. As it melts, spoon the foaming butter over the fish to baste. Fry for another minute until the fish is just cooked through. Remove from the heat and transfer to a warm plate, reserving the excess butter and oil. Leave the fish to rest for a couple of minutes.

Meanwhile, reheat the beans if necessary, and stir through the chopped parsley. Season to taste with black pepper. (You probably won't need salt because of the bacon and haddock.) Spoon the beans on to warm plates and lay the smoked haddock fillets on top. Spoon over the crispy bacon and a little oil and butter from the pan in which you cooked the fish, garnish with parsley leaves and serve at once.

SERVES 4

White beans and parsley:
800g soaked white beans (cannellini or haricot blanc)
80g bacon trimmings or 3 rashers of smoked streaky bacon
few sprigs of thyme
half a head of garlic, sliced horizontally
handful of flat-leaf parsley, leaves chopped

Smoked haddock:
2 thick rashers of smoked streaky bacon, chopped
3 tbsp olive oil
2 fillets of undyed smoked haddock (about 600g), skinned
few knobs of butter
few sprigs of thyme
handful of flat-leaf parsley, leaves picked

Gordon's posh kedgeree

I've cooked many versions of kedgeree in my life. This upmarket version is the one I make when we have guests staying over the weekend. It makes a great Saturday or Sunday morning brunch, as rice is the ultimate treat if you've got a hangover.

SERVES 4–6

675ml chicken or fish stock (see page 258 or 262)
few sprigs of thyme
pinch of saffron strands
260g skinless lightly smoked salmon fillets
200g raw king prawns, peeled and deveined
2 tbsp olive oil

2 banana shallots, finely chopped
few knobs of butter
1 tsp mild curry powder
350g basmati rice
12 quail's eggs, at room temperature
handful of flat-leaf parsley, leaves chopped
lemon wedges, to garnish

Put the stock, thyme, saffron and a pinch of salt and pepper into a saucepan. Bring to a simmer, then gently lower the salmon fillets into the stock and poach for 4 minutes. Lift them out with a fish slice or slotted spoon on to a warm plate. Add the prawns to the stock and poach for about 2 minutes, just until they turn firm and opaque. Using a slotted spoon, transfer the prawns to the plate of salmon, cover with foil and keep warm.

Strain the stock into a measuring jug and discard the thyme. Return the pan to the heat and add the olive oil, shallots and some seasoning. Fry for about 4–6 minutes, stirring occasionally, until the shallots are soft but not browned. Add the butter and curry powder. Stir for 2 minutes, then tip in the rice. Stir and cook for another couple of minutes to lightly toast the rice.

Add a generous pinch of salt and pepper and pour in the stock. Give the mixture one more stir and bring to a simmer. Cover the pan with a lid and set the timer to 10 minutes. When 10 minutes is up, and without lifting the lid, turn off the heat and let the rice stand for 5 minutes.

Meanwhile, boil the quail's eggs in a small saucepan for 3 minutes. Drain and refresh under cold running water. Crack and peel off the skins, then cut each egg in half.

Fluff the rice with a fork to separate the grains, then taste and adjust the seasoning, adding a knob of butter if you wish. Break the salmon fillet into large flakes and add to the rice, along with the prawns and most of the chopped parsley. Gently mix the ingredients through the rice. Pile on to warm plates and garnish with the quail's eggs, remaining parsley and lemon wedges. Serve at once.

Spinach, mushroom and ricotta cannelloni

Like the grilled vegetable lasagne (see page 56), this is another delicious dish that's definitely not just for the vegetarians. It can be prepared in advance and then put in the oven for about 20 minutes when you're ready to eat.

First, prepare the sauce. Melt the butter in a saucepan and stir in the flour, mustard and cayenne pepper. Stir over low heat for 2–3 minutes. Slowly whisk in the milk and continue to stir until smooth. Simmer and stir for another 5 minutes to cook out the flour. Remove the pan from the heat and stir in the cheeses until they have melted and the sauce is smooth. Transfer to a bowl and leave to cool. Once cooled, stir in the crème fraiche to loosen the consistency. Taste and adjust the seasoning.

To prepare the filling, melt the butter in a pan and add the spinach, some seasoning and a light grating of nutmeg. Cook over high heat until the spinach has wilted, then tip into a colander set over a large bowl and leave to cool. Return the pan to the heat and add the olive oil, mushrooms and some seasoning. Sauté the mushrooms for 3–4 minutes until tender and any juices released have been cooked off. Transfer to a large bowl and leave to cool. Give the spinach a light squeeze to remove excess moisture and add to the mushrooms. Stir in the ricotta and parmesan. Taste and adjust the seasoning.

Roll the cannelloni one at a time. Place a lasagne sheet on a chopping board. Spoon 2 tablespoons of filling along one end, leaving a bit of space at both edges, and roll up. Place on a tray, joined-side down, and repeat with the remaining pasta and filling.

Preheat the oven to 220°C/Gas 7. Spread half the cheese sauce over the base of a large ovenproof dish and arrange the cannelloni in a single layer on top. Spread the remaining sauce over to cover the cannelloni, then sprinkle with the parmesan. Bake for 15–20 minutes until the topping is golden brown. Bring to the table and serve at once.

SERVES 6
300g fresh lasagne sheets (about 12)
2–3 tbsp freshly grated parmesan

Filling:
15g butter
400g spinach leaves, washed
nutmeg, for grating
2–3 tbsp olive oil
500g portabella mushrooms (or mixture of wild mushrooms), sliced
400g ricotta
2 tbsp grated parmesan

Cheese sauce:
20g butter
20g plain flour
1 tsp English mustard
pinch of cayenne pepper
300ml whole milk
60g mild cheddar, finely grated
2 tbsp freshly grated parmesan
200ml crème fraiche or double cream

Goat's cheese, beetroot and lentil salad

Baking beetroot in a salt crust intensifies the flavour. This salad combines sweet roasted beetroot with earthy puy lentils and creamy goat's cheese. The marinated beetroot slices are optional, but they do add to the beauty of the salad. (Illustrated on page 73.)

SERVES 4

Baked beetroot:
400–450g regular or mixed beetroot of
   similar size (such as golden or cheltenham)
rock salt or coarse sea salt
stripped leaves from a few sprigs of thyme

Lentils:
150g umbrian castelluccio or
   puy lentils, rinsed and drained
80g bacon trimmings
1 carrot
2 celery stalks
few sprigs of thyme

Marinated beetroot (optional):
2 baby beetroot, preferably candy, chioggia
   or pablo varieties
6 tbsp extra virgin olive oil
3 tbsp balsamic vinegar

To serve:
handful of mixed salad leaves
handful each of flat-leaf parsley and mint,
   leaves chopped
200g goat's cheese, crumbled or chopped

Preheat the oven to 180°C/Gas 4. Wash and dry the beetroot, then trim off the tops. Spread a thin layer of rock salt on a large piece of foil. Scatter over the thyme leaves and put the beetroot in the middle. Bring up the edges of the foil to seal the beetroot and salt. Bake for about 30–40 minutes until tender when pierced with a small sharp knife.

Prepare the lentils by putting all the ingredients in a pan with water to cover by 4–5cm. Bring to a simmer and cook for 15–20 minutes until the lentils are tender. When cooked, drain the lentils. Discard the bacon, vegetables and thyme sprigs. Meanwhile, if making the marinated beetroot, peel and thinly slice it with a mandolin and place in a bowl. Drizzle over the olive oil and balsamic vinegar and season. Chill and leave to marinate for at least 15–20 minutes.

Unwrap the beetroot parcel and allow some of the heat to disperse. While the beetroot is still warm, peel it using a small knife (wearing a pair of gloves to avoid staining your hands). Cut into quarters, and divide between individual serving plates along with the lentils. Garnish each plate with the marinated beetroot slices, if using. Add a scattering of salad leaves, herbs and goat's cheese to serve.

Wild mushroom barley risotto

Pearl barley adds a nutty flavour to this risotto, and it provides an interesting base for wild mushrooms. It's very easy to cook with – no way as high-maintenance as risotto rice – as you can leave it to simmer away without needing to stir it constantly.

Clean the mushrooms and thickly slice the large ones. Set aside while you start the risotto.

Bring the stock to a gentle simmer in a medium saucepan. Heat the butter and a tablespoon of olive oil in a large saucepan or sauté pan and add the onion and a pinch of salt and pepper. Gently fry the onion, stirring occasionally, for 4–6 minutes until it begins to soften. Tip in the barley and stir well to coat. Toast the barley for 2 minutes, stirring frequently.

Pour in the splash of wine and let it bubble until reduced by half. Stir in two-thirds of the hot stock and let the barley simmer, stirring every once in a while, until it has absorbed almost all the liquid. Add more stock, a ladleful at a time, and simmer until the barley is just tender. (You may not need all the stock.) Stir in the parmesan and mascarpone and season well to taste. Remove the pan from the heat and cover with a lid to keep warm.

Heat the remaining oil in a large frying pan. Fry the mushrooms with some seasoning until they are lightly browned and any moisture released has been cooked off. It should take about 3–4 minutes. Add the mushrooms to the risotto and stir well to mix.

Divide the risotto among warm plates and sprinkle over the chopped parsley. Serve immediately.

SERVES 4

400g wild mushrooms (such as ceps, trompettes de la mort, chanterelles and girolles)
900ml chicken or vegetable stock (see pages 258–9)
20g butter
3 tbsp olive oil
1 onion, finely chopped
200g pearl barley
splash of dry white wine
25g freshly grated parmesan
2 tbsp mascarpone
handful of flat-leaf parsley, leaves finely chopped

Herby rice pilaf with pistachios and almonds

This sweetly perfumed rice pilaf is ideal with a good curry (see the goat curry on page 122) or with baked fish.

Preheat the oven to 190°C/Gas 5. Cut a circle of greaseproof paper slightly larger than a heavy-based ovenproof pan or a cast-iron casserole. Snip a small hole in the middle of the paper to serve as a steam vent.

Heat the pan with the oil and sauté the onion for 4–6 minutes until it begins to soften. Stir in the rice, cinnamon, star anise, lemon and orange zests, and some salt and pepper. Stir well and toast the rice for a couple of minutes. Pour in the hot water and bring to the boil. Take the pan off the heat and quickly cover with the greaseproof paper before transferring to the oven.

Bake for 20–25 minutes until the rice is tender and has absorbed most of the water. Remove the pan from the oven and allow to stand for about 5 minutes. Discard the greaseproof paper and fork the rice to separate the grains. Taste and adjust the seasoning, then stir through the chopped nuts and herbs.

SERVES 4
3 tbsp olive oil
1 Spanish onion, chopped
250g basmati rice
1 cinnamon stick
3 star anise
**pared zest of 1 lemon and
    1 orange**
525ml hot water
**75g toasted almonds and
    pistachios, roughly
    chopped**
**large handful of mixed
    herbs, such as flat-leaf
    parsley, coriander, mint,
    chervil and chives, leaves
    chopped**

fish
and shellfish

To cook good food, you need to start with the best quality ingredients you can find. This is paramount when it comes to fish and shellfish. We are fortunate to live near a fantastic fishmonger, Moxon's, in Clapham South. The shop is tiny, but it stocks a variety of incredibly fresh seafood. Whenever we get the chance, Tana and I take the kids with us, as we feel it is important for them to see the amazing diversity of seafood on offer. They are growing up knowing what a brill is, what red mullet and sardines look like.

Sustainable fishing is an issue that is important to me. Over recent years, I've been trying to encourage the use of less expensive but sustainable fish, such as herrings, mackerel, whiting and trout. Of course I also enjoy cooking and eating scallops, oysters, halibut and sea bass, but only every once in a while. The idea is to be conscious of what you buy and vary what you cook to keep things different and exciting.

Fish curry with lime and coconut rice
Breaded and fried oysters with sauce gribiche
Smoked trout pâté with horseradish cream and melba toasts
Whiting in piquant tomato sauce
Stuffed bream wrapped with bacon
Thai-style fishcakes with sweet chilli sauce
Clams with old spot bacon
Sea bass with olives, tomatoes and fennel
Grilled herrings with harissa
Red mullet with tomatoes, olives and anchovies
Fisherman's stew
Poached halibut with creamy white wine and tarragon sauce
Devilled mackerel with tomato and fennel salad and horseradish potatoes
Grilled scallop and prawn brochettes with coriander and chilli butter

Fish curry with lime and coconut rice

I was inspired to make this curry after a glorious holiday in Thailand, where we ate spicy Thai food for breakfast, lunch and dinner. Any combination of fish and shellfish will work for this curry, though firm-textured fish that won't disintegrate as it cooks is best. Chunks of red snapper, hake or bream are all good; you can leave the skins on to prevent the fish from breaking up. (Illustrated on page 83.)

SERVES 4

Fish curry:
400g monkfish fillets, pin-boned
   and cut into bite-size chunks
400ml coconut milk, mixed with 400ml water
500g live mussels
1 tbsp palm sugar
2½ tbsp fish sauce
150g sugarsnap peas
3–4 spring onions, finely chopped
handful of basil or coriander leaves,
   to garnish
2 tbsp groundnut oil

Curry paste:
3 garlic cloves, roughly chopped
3 large shallots, roughly chopped
6–7 large mild red chillies,
   deseeded and chopped
5cm piece of ginger, roughly chopped
small handful of coriander stems, chopped
1 lemongrass stalk, finely chopped
2 kaffir lime leaves, finely chopped (or finely
   grated zest of 2 limes)
½ tsp ground coriander
½ tsp ground cumin
¼ tsp ground turmeric
3–4 tbsp water

Lime and coconut rice:
300g Thai fragrant rice, washed and drained
200ml coconut milk, mixed with 200ml water
juice of 1 lime
2 kaffir lime leaves
pinch of sea salt
toasted coconut shavings, to garnish
   (optional)

Put the monkfish pieces into a large bowl with a little salt and pepper and spoon over a few tablespoons of coconut milk. Cover with cling film and chill until ready to cook. Wash the mussels and discard any that do not open when gently tapped.

To make the lime and coconut rice, put all the ingredients – except for the coconut shavings – into a medium saucepan. Bring to the boil, then reduce the heat and cover the pan. Simmer for 8–10 minutes until the rice has absorbed most of the liquid. Without removing the lid, turn off the heat and leave the rice to steam for 5–10 minutes.

While the rice is cooking, put all the ingredients for the curry paste into a food processor and whiz to a smooth paste, stopping the machine once or twice to scrape down the sides. As necessary, add a little more water to get a finely ground paste.

Heat the oil in a deep pan or a wok. Add the curry paste and stir-fry for about 2–3 minutes over low heat, just until the paste smells fragrant. Pour in the coconut milk and water, then stir in the palm sugar and fish sauce. Bring the liquid to a simmer, stirring to dissolve the sugar.

Tip in the sugarsnap peas and cook for 2 minutes. Add the mussels and fish to the pan, cover and simmer for another 2–3 minutes until the mussels have opened and the fish is opaque and just cooked through. Scatter over the spring onions and basil or coriander leaves. Serve immediately with the lime and coconut rice, garnished with a sprinkling of toasted coconut shavings.

Breaded and fried oysters with sauce gribiche

Crisp breaded oysters are a good choice for those who are averse to eating them raw. I serve mine with sauce gribiche, which is similar to tartare sauce, but with the addition of finely chopped boiled egg. Great to have with a glass of chilled white wine or champagne.

First, prepare the sauce. Put the egg into a small saucepan and cover with cold water. Bring to the boil, then lower the heat and simmer for 9 minutes. Drain and cool under cold running water. Peel and halve the egg, then scoop out the yolk into the bowl of a food processor. Finely chop the white and set aside. Add the mustard, vinegar, olive oil, capers and a little salt and pepper to the food processor and whiz for a few seconds. Transfer to a bowl and stir in the egg whites and parsley. Taste and adjust the seasoning. Spoon into a serving bowl and set aside.

Shuck the oysters one at a time. Hold an oyster in a thick folded tea towel in one hand and take an oyster knife in the other. Stick the knife through the hinge of the oyster, holding it level, then wriggle the knife from side to side to cut through the strong hinge muscle. Push in the knife and twist up to lift the top shell. Pick out any large pieces of shell, then slide the knife along the bottom shell to release the oyster flesh. Tip the flesh and juice into a sieve set over a bowl.

Mix the flour with some salt and pepper in a wide bowl. Place the beaten egg in another wide bowl, and the breadcrumbs in a third. Toss the oysters in the seasoned flour and shake off any excess. Dip into the beaten egg, then coat evenly with the breadcrumbs. Arrange on a plate and set aside. Heat 3–4cm of oil in a small saucepan until hot. (A little piece of bread should sizzle vigorously when dropped in.) Fry the breaded oysters in 2 or 3 batches for just a few seconds until evenly golden brown and crisp. Drain on a plate lined with kitchen paper. Serve immediately with the sauce gribiche on the side.

SERVES 4 AS A STARTER
Breaded oysters:
20 fresh oysters
60g plain flour
1 large egg, lightly beaten
60g Japanese panko breadcrumbs
groundnut or vegetable oil, for deep-frying

Sauce gribiche:
1 large egg
1 tbsp dijon mustard
1 tbsp white wine vinegar
120ml light olive oil
1 tbsp capers, rinsed and drained
1 tbsp chopped flat-leaf parsley

Smoked trout pâté with horseradish cream and melba toasts

This easy, prepare-ahead starter is ideal for entertaining. Make the smoked trout pâté a day ahead and chill it. The melba toasts can be made several days earlier, as they store well in an airtight container. When your guests have arrived, all you have to do is to dress and garnish some salad leaves with cold smoked trout, then bring everything to the table.

SERVES 4
Smoked trout pâté:
200g hot-smoked trout
100ml crème fraiche
100ml double cream
1 tbsp creamed horseradish
squeeze of lemon juice, to taste
small handful of dill, chopped, 4 small sprigs reserved for garnish

To serve:
8 slices white or brown bread
8 slices cold smoked trout
few handfuls of salad leaves

Put all the ingredients for the pâté into a food processor and pulse until well mixed. Leave the mixture coarse for a rustic texture. Season to taste with freshly ground black pepper, then spoon into individual ramekins or ceramic pots and garnish each with a sprig of dill.

To make the melba toasts, preheat the grill to high and toast the bread lightly on both sides. Cut off the crusts, then, holding the toast flat against a chopping board, slide the knife between the toasted edges to split the bread horizontally. Cut the split bread into triangles and arrange on a baking sheet with the untoasted sides up. Place under the grill until the triangles are golden and crisp and the edges have curled slightly.

Serve with the individual pots of pâté and a couple of slices of smoked trout draped over a handful of salad leaves.

Whiting in piquant tomato sauce

This is one of the easiest and healthiest ways to cook fish. Make a delicious sauce, place the fish fillets on top, cover and steam. The sauce can be made in advance, then the fish needs only a few minutes to cook. Saffron rice or crushed new potatoes are ideal accompaniments.

Trim the fish fillets to neaten the edges, then remove any pin-bones with a pair of kitchen tweezers. Chill until just about ready to serve.

Heat the oil in a wide, heavy-based pan over low-to-medium heat. Stir in the onion and a pinch each of salt and pepper. Cook for 4–6 minutes until the onion begins to soften, then add the chopped garlic and anchovy and fry for 1–2 minutes more. Pour in a splash of white wine and let it simmer until the pan is quite dry, then stir in the stock, tomatoes, chilli and oregano. Leave to simmer for about 30 minutes until the tomatoes have broken down and the sauce has thickened. Taste and adjust the seasoning, adding a pinch of sugar and a few dashes of Tabasco sauce to taste.

When ready to serve, season the fish fillets with salt and pepper, then lower into the pan of tomato sauce and cover with a tight-fitting lid. Steam the fish over medium heat for 3–4 minutes until it is just firm and opaque.

Lift the fish out with a fish slice and serve with generous spoonfuls of piquant tomato sauce and a sprinkling of basil leaves.

SERVES 4

4 whiting fillets, about 150g each
2 tbsp olive oil
1 large onion, finely chopped
3 garlic cloves, finely chopped
2 anchovy fillets in olive oil, finely chopped
splash of dry white wine
100ml fish or chicken stock (see page 262 or 258) or water
400g tin chopped tomatoes
pinch of dried chilli flakes
½ tsp dried oregano
pinch of caster sugar
few dashes of Tabasco sauce
basil leaves, to serve

Stuffed bream wrapped with bacon

Stuffing fish with forcemeat, or in my case sausagemeat, is a classic idea that even featured in Mrs Beeton's recipes in the 1800s. I find wrapping the bream with thin slices of bacon not only holds in the stuffing, but also imparts a smoky and savoury flavour to the fish.

SERVES 2
2 medium whole bream, scaled and gutted
20 thin rashers of smoked streaky bacon
olive oil, to drizzle
few sprigs of thyme
4 cloves garlic, skins on and halved
lemon wedges, to serve (optional)

Forcemeat:
200g sausagemeat (or 2 sausages with skins removed)
leaves from a sprig of thyme
small handful each of flat-leaf parsley and chives, chopped
pinch of cayenne pepper
few drops of lemon juice

Preheat the oven to 220ºC/Gas 7. Mix together all the ingredients for the forcemeat stuffing and set aside.

Clean the fish and pat dry with kitchen paper. Rub all over with a little salt and pepper, then stuff the gutted cavities of each bream with the forcemeat.

Flatten the bacon between sheets of baking parchment if it is quite thick. For each fish, take 10 rashers and lay them out in chevrons on a chopping board, crossing each pair over at the base of its 'V'. Put the fish in the middle and wrap the bacon rashers round it to secure the forcemeat, alternating left and right.

Place the stuffed, wrapped fish on 1 large or 2 smaller baking trays. Drizzle with olive oil and scatter over the sea salt, thyme and garlic halves. Bake for about 25–30 minutes, turning over halfway, until the bacon is golden brown and crisp and the fish is cooked through. Serve with lemon wedges, if you like.

Thai-style fishcakes with sweet chilli sauce

These light and flavoursome fishcakes are a doddle to make, and they don't require coating in breadcrumbs. Authentic Thai recipes include finely chopped long beans (also known as yard beans), but you have to visit an Asian grocer to get them. Tender young French beans make good alternatives, as they don't require pre-blanching. You can buy sweet chilli sauce in the supermarket, but the best one will be the one you make yourself.

SERVES 4

225g skinless white fish fillets, such as hake, ling or coley
225g peeled prawns, deveined and roughly chopped
1 tbsp Thai red curry paste (to make this yourself, see page 80)
100ml coconut milk
finely grated zest of 1 lime
small handful of coriander, finely chopped
2 tbsp fish sauce
1 tsp palm or light brown sugar
60g fine French beans, very finely sliced into rounds
1 spring onion, finely sliced into rounds
2–3 tbsp plain flour
groundnut or sunflower oil, for frying

Sweet chilli sauce:
5 tbsp caster sugar
3 garlic cloves, roughly chopped
4cm piece of ginger, roughly chopped
small handful of coriander leaves
3 long red chillies, deseeded and roughly chopped
juice of 1 large lime
1 tbsp fish sauce
1 tbsp light soy sauce

First, make the sweet chilli sauce. Place the sugar in a small heavy-based saucepan with 3–4 tablespoons of water. Stir to dissolve the sugar, then bring to the boil for 5–8 minutes until the syrup has caramelized to a light golden colour.

Meanwhile, place the garlic, ginger, coriander leaves, chillies and lime juice in a food processor and whiz to a coarse paste. When the sugar syrup has reached a light golden caramel colour, carefully add the wet paste, standing well back, as the caramel will sputter and spit. Stir in the fish and soy sauces. Return to a simmer, stirring frequently to dissolve any caramel that has hardened, then immediately take the pan off the heat. Leave to cool completely before spooning into individual dipping bowls.

To make the fishcakes, cut the fish into rough chunks, discarding any bones you come across, then put in a food processor with the prawns. Add the curry paste, coconut, lime zest, coriander, fish sauce, sugar and a little salt and pepper. Pulse to a rough and sticky paste – don't over-process the fish – then transfer to a bowl and stir in the chopped French beans and spring onions.

Put the flour into a shallow dish. Divide the fish mixture up into 12 or 16 pieces. With wet hands, roll each piece into a ball, then flatten into a round patty and coat lightly with the flour. Heat 2cm of oil in a wide frying pan and fry the fishcakes in batches for 1–1½ minutes on each side or until golden brown. Drain each batch on kitchen paper and repeat with the remainder. Serve the fishcakes warm, with the sweet chilli sauce for dipping.

Clams with old spot bacon

This surf-and-turf starter is a regular feature on my pub menus. You can use any good-quality bacon, but for outstanding flavour, try Gloucester old spot. I generally use carpetshell clams (also known as palourdes) at the restaurants, but any variety will do, as long as the clams are very fresh. Serve with crusty bread on the side to soak up the savoury juices.

Wash the clams and discard any that do not shut tightly when gently tapped.

Place a large heavy-based pan (with lid) over medium heat. Add the oil, bacon and thyme and fry for 4–5 minutes until the bacon is golden brown around the edges. Increase the heat, pour in a splash of white wine and immediately tip in the clams. Give the pan a shake, then cover the pan. Let steam for 3–4 minutes until the clams have opened. (Discard any that do not.)

Grate over some black pepper and add a squeeze of lemon juice, if you like. You probably won't need to add salt, as the clams and bacon are already salty. Divide the clams, bacon and pan juices among warm bowls and serve at once.

SERVES 4 AS A STARTER
2kg clams
2 tbsp olive oil
250g bacon slab, cut into thick 3–4cm chunks
few sprigs of thyme
splash of dry white wine
squeeze of lemon juice (optional)

Sea bass with olives, tomatoes and fennel

This is a delicious and healthy way of cooking whole sea bass. It takes me back to my younger days, when I worked aboard a luxury yacht as a private chef. I made elegant and sophisticated dishes for the guests, but staff meals had to be quick, easy and satisfying. Dishes like this one made me very popular among the crew. Serve with new potatoes on the side.

SERVES 4

2 whole small sea bass, about 400–450g each, scaled and gutted
2 tbsp olive oil, plus extra to rub over the fish
1 large or 2 medium fennel bulbs, thinly sliced
splash of dry white wine
10 plum tomatoes, peeled and roughly chopped
60g pitted black olives, drained and sliced
handful of basil or dill, roughly chopped

Clean the fish and pat dry with kitchen paper. Score the fish several times on each side, then rub all over with olive oil. Sprinkle with a little salt and pepper and set aside.

Preheat the oven to 200°C/Gas 6 and heat the oil in an ovenproof pan that is wide enough to fit the fish. Add the fennel and a little seasoning. Sauté the fennel for about 5 minutes until it begins to soften. Pour in a generous splash of wine, then stir in the tomatoes and olives. Scatter over half the basil and dill, then rest the sea bass on top of the sauce.

Transfer the pan to the oven and bake for 15–20 minutes until the fish is just cooked through – it should be opaque at the thickest part of the flesh. Serve the fish and sauce straight from the pan.

Grilled herrings with harissa

Harissa is traditionally made with recon-
stituted dried chillies, garlic, various ground
spices, mint and olive oil. I prefer to make
mine with fresh chillies, sweet roasted red
peppers and a splash of vinegar to give the
sauce a fresh zing – a perfect contrast to
rich, oily fish such as herrings. Any extras
keep well in the fridge, covered with a thin
layer of olive oil.

Lightly score the herrings on both sides, then season all over with
salt and pepper. Oil a baking tray and arrange the lemon slices over
the base. Place the fish on top of the lemon slices and drizzle over
with a little olive oil and lemon juice. Sprinkle over a little more
seasoning and chill while you prepare the sauce.

Split the chillies in half lengthways and scrape off the seeds.
Roughly chop the flesh and put into a small food processor or
blender. Core, deseed and roughly chop the roasted red pepper.
Add to the chillies. Put the rest of the ingredients, except the sugar,
into the food processor with a little seasoning to taste. Whiz until
smooth, stopping the machine to scrape down the sides of the
processor once or twice. Taste and adjust the seasoning, adding a
pinch of sugar as necessary, to balance out the flavour.

When ready to cook, preheat the grill to the highest setting. Place
the herrings under the grill and cook for about 3 minutes on each
side. Transfer to warm plates and serve immediately, with the
harissa and some natural yoghurt on the side.

SERVES 4
Grilled herrings:
4 whole herrings, scaled
    and gutted
olive oil
1 lemon, thinly sliced
squeeze of lemon juice
natural yoghurt, to serve

Harissa:
3 large red chillies
1 roasted red pepper in
    brine, drained
2 garlic cloves, roughly
    chopped
pinch of saffron strands
1 tsp ground coriander
1 tsp ground cumin
1 tsp tomato purée
1 tsp red wine vinegar
3 tbsp olive oil
pinch of caster sugar
    (optional)

Red mullet with tomatoes, olives and anchovies

A beautifully simple dish with Mediterranean flavours. Ask your fishmonger to butterfly the mullets so that each fish is boned and opened out flat, its two fillets still held together by its skin – unless, of course, you are adept at doing this yourself.

SERVES 4

4 large red mullets, about 300g each,
   scaled, gutted and butterflied
   (ask your fishmonger to do this)
4 tbsp olive oil
200g cherry tomatoes, halved
100g pitted black olives (about 20), sliced
3 anchovies in olive oil
squeeze of lemon juice
handful of basil, leaves roughly chopped

Clean the fish and pat dry with kitchen paper. Heat a large frying pan with the oil until hot. Season the fish and fry for 1½ minutes, skin-side down. Turn over and cook the other side for 1–1½ minutes. Remove to a plate and keep warm.

Tip the cherry tomatoes into the pan and add the olives and anchovies. Toss over high heat for a couple of minutes, adding a squeeze of lemon juice, and cook until the tomatoes have softened slightly. Toss in the basil and immediately divide between warm serving plates. Place the fish on top, skin-side up, and serve at once.

Fisherman's stew

The variety of seafood here adds to the complexity of the stew. You could keep to just two types – a firm white fish with some clams, perhaps – but the crabmeat enriches and thickens the sauce at the end and is well worth including. Lots of good crusty bread is a must, and the stew is also delicious over pasta or with boiled new potatoes.

Wash the clams and mussels and discard any that do not shut tightly when gently tapped. Put the wine and bouquet garni in a large heavy-based pan (with a tight-fitting lid) and bring to the boil. As soon as it starts to boil, tip in the clams and mussels. Give the mixture a stir, then cover and steam for 2–3 minutes until the clams and mussels have opened.

Tip the shellfish into a colander set over a large bowl to collect the liquid. Discard the bouquet garni. Return the pan to the heat and add the olive oil, leek and fennel. Sauté for about 4–5 minutes, then pour in the liquid from the clams and mussels. Add the fish stock and saffron and bring to a simmer. Let it cook until reduced by a third, then pour in the cream.

Meanwhile, extract the flesh from most of the clams and mussels, discarding any that have not opened, and keeping back a few of each in their shells to use as garnish.

Five minutes before you are ready to serve, bring the stock back to a simmer. Add the prawns and cook for 2 minutes, then add the fish and crabmeat. Poach for another minute, just until the fish turns opaque. Return the clams and mussels to the pan to warm through. Remove the pan from the heat. Ladle the stew into warm bowls and garnish with a little chopped parsley.

SERVES 4
500g clams
500g mussels
100ml dry white wine or Noilly Prat
1 bouquet garni (1 bay leaf, sprig of parsley and thyme and 2 blades of mace tied together)
2 tbsp olive oil
2 large leeks, finely sliced
1 medium fennel bulb, finely sliced
700ml fish stock (see page 262)
pinch of saffron strands
100ml double cream
200g king prawns
400g plaice fillet, with skin on, in bite-size chunks
200g crabmeat
small handful of flat-leaf parsley, leaves chopped

Poached halibut with creamy white wine and tarragon sauce

Halibut has a delicate flavour, and is perfectly matched with this creamy white wine and tarragon sauce. The sauce can be made in advance, but I wouldn't bother to precook the fish – after all, it doesn't take long to poach, and you'll need a few minutes to reheat the sauce and prepare any side dishes. To complete the meal, serve with root vegetables and some wilted spinach.

SERVES 4

Poached halibut:
1 bay leaf
few sprigs of thyme
½ tsp black peppercorns
½ lemon, sliced into rounds
large pinch of rock salt
4 x 150g skinless and boneless halibut fillets

White wine and tarragon sauce:
2 tbsp olive oil
3 large shallots, finely chopped
125ml dry white wine
300ml fish stock (see page 262)
250ml double cream
lemon juice, to taste
handful of tarragon, leaves chopped

First, make the sauce. Heat the oil in a medium saucepan and add the shallots and some seasoning. Sweat the shallots for 5–6 minutes until soft and without colouring. Deglaze the pan with the white wine and let it boil until the pan is quite dry.

Add the fish stock, bring to the boil and reduce by half. Finally, pour in the double cream, return to the boil and cook until thickened to pouring-cream consistency. Strain through a sieve into a clean pan and adjust the seasoning with salt, pepper and a little lemon juice. Keep warm and stir in the tarragon leaves just before serving.

Poach the halibut as you are ready to serve. Put all the aromatics into a large saucepan and half fill the pan with water. Bring to the boil. Reduce the heat to a simmer. Season the fish with salt and pepper, then lower into the liquid. Gently poach for 8–10 minutes until the fish is opaque and just firm.

Carefully remove the halibut fillets with a fish slice and dab dry with kitchen paper. Place on warmed plates and pour over the white wine and tarragon sauce.

Devilled mackerel with tomato and fennel salad and horseradish potatoes

In my opinion, we don't eat enough mackerel in this country. It is abundant, cheap and full of healthy fats. The 'devilled' butter in this recipe gives the fish a sweet, smoky and slightly spicy edge. You could also use it with mackerel fillets: they'll obviously need less time to cook. Tomato and fennel salad and horseradish potatoes are fantastic accompaniments. (Illustrated on page 104.)

SERVES 4
4 whole mackerel, scaled and gutted
100g butter, softened to room temperature
1 tsp cayenne pepper
2 tsp sweet smoked paprika
1 tsp ground coriander
1 tbsp golden caster sugar
½ tsp dry English mustard
2 tsp red or white wine vinegar

Horseradish potatoes:
500g new potatoes, washed and halved if large
2 shallots, finely chopped
2 tbsp sour cream
2 tbsp horseradish cream
few sprigs of dill, roughly chopped

Tomato and fennel salad:
1 large fennel bulb
2 ripe plum tomatoes
handful of flat-leaf parsley, leaves roughly chopped
few sprigs of dill, roughly chopped
½ tsp caster sugar
juice of ½ lemon
3 tbsp olive oil

First, make the horseradish potatoes. Cook the potatoes in salted water for 10–12 minutes, until tender when pierced with a sharp knife. Drain into a large bowl and cool slightly. Stir in the shallot, sour cream and horseradish cream and season to taste with salt and pepper. Finally, stir the dill through. Set aside to serve warm or at room temperature.

For the fennel salad, trim off the base of the fennel, then shave into very thin slices using a mandolin. Immerse the slices in a bowl of iced water and leave to soak and crisp up for about 10 minutes. Meanwhile, cut the tomatoes into thin wedges. Put the tomatoes into a large bowl along with the drained fennel and add the chopped herbs. Mix together the caster sugar, lemon juice and olive oil for the dressing, along with some salt and pepper, pour it over the tomatoes and fennel and mix well. Let the flavours infuse for 10–15 minutes before serving.

Heat the grill to the highest setting. Slash each mackerel in 2cm increments on both sides, then place on a baking dish. Mix all the remaining ingredients together in a bowl to get a thick spiced butter, seasoning well with salt and pepper. Rub the butter all over the mackerel, including inside the cavity. If the butter firms up on contact with the chilled fish and you find it difficult to spread, then slightly melt it in a saucepan and pour it over instead.

Grill the mackerel for 4–5 minutes on each side until the fish is just firm and cooked through.

Serve immediately with the tomato and fennel salad and horseradish potatoes.

Grilled scallop and prawn brochettes with coriander and chilli butter

These are lovely, and fun to eat with your fingers. Take care not to overcook the scallops and prawns or they'll turn rubbery. The recipe makes more coriander and chilli butter than you need. It keeps for about a week in the fridge and is also good with grilled meats and fish.

SERVES 4

Scallop and prawn brochettes:
2–3 tbsp olive oil
sprig of rosemary, leaves finely chopped
small handful of flat-leaf parsley,
    leaves chopped
juice and zest of ½ lemon
12 large scallops
12 king prawns, peeled and deveined

Coriander and chilli butter:
125g butter, softened to room temperature
finely grated zest of 1 lemon
1 small red chilli, trimmed, deseeded and
    finely chopped
small handful of coriander, leaves chopped
1 large garlic clove, finely crushed

First, prepare the coriander and chilli butter. Place all the ingredients in a bowl along with a generous pinch of salt and pepper. Beat with a fork until well combined. Spoon the butter along the length of a large sheet of cling film. Roll up the cling film to shape the butter into a log. Holding the sides of the cling film, roll the log on the work surface to even out the thickness. Chill for a few hours until firm.

Meanwhile, soak 12 bamboo skewers in cold water. This will help to prevent them from burning too quickly during grilling.

Mix the olive oil, chopped herbs, lemon juice and zest together in a bowl and set aside. Thread 2 scallops and 2 prawns alternately on each skewer, then brush with the lemon and herb marinade. Place the skewers on a tray, cover with cling film and chill for 20–30 minutes.

Prepare the barbecue or heat a griddle pan until hot. Season the scallops and prawns with salt and pepper. Barbecue or griddle for 1½–2 minutes on each side, basting occasionally with any leftover marinade, until the scallops and prawns are opaque and lightly charred. Remove to a serving plate and top with slices of the coriander and chilli butter. Serve immediately.

meat
and poultry

While we may use expensive cuts of meat and poultry at the restaurants, at home I'm more interested in cooking with less popular cuts. It is more exciting and challenging to convert cheap cuts of meat or ordinary chicken legs into something appealing and scrumptious than it is to grill a piece of fillet steak. The cheaper cuts usually require slow-cooking methods, such as poaching, braising and stewing, to tenderize them. A long and gentle cooking process is also an opportunity to infuse the meat with extra flavour.

As you can see from this chapter, I sometimes like to add a sweet element to meat and poultry dishes. Fresh or dried fruit can help to cut the richness of the meat.

Poached rabbit legs with gremolata
Pork fillet stroganoff
Home-made bangers
Classic mixed grill
Angus beef olives
Corn-fed chicken legs with braised peas and onions
Goat curry
Roast loin of pork with Bramley apple sauce
Sweet potato and duck rösti with fried duck eggs
Honey roast ham
Cider and honey roast leg of lamb
Lamb shank cassoulet
Roast rib-eye with caramelized shallot and red wine gravy
Lamb stew with bacon, sweet onions and prunes
Braised chicken legs with honey and five-spice
Duck breasts with port and cherry sauce

Poached rabbit legs with gremolata

Rabbit legs benefit from slow cooking, and this is also one of the simplest ways to cook them – gently poached in a light and delicate broth. For a deeper-flavoured broth, use home-made chicken stock instead of water. You could also add chunks of potatoes or some pearl barley to bulk up the dish for a rustic one-pot meal. Serve with warm chunks of baguette or pain de campagne.

SERVES 4
4 rabbit legs (hindquarters)
2 large carrots, cut into large chunks
1 Spanish onion, roughly chopped
1 large leek, cut into large chunks
2 celery stalks, cut into large chunks
half a head of garlic, cut horizontally
handful of thyme
1 bay leaf
½ tsp black peppercorns
½ tsp coriander seeds

Gremolata:
100ml olive oil
2 garlic cloves, finely grated
grated zest and juice of 1 lemon
handful of flat-leaf parsley, chopped

Season the rabbit legs well and put them in a cast-iron or heavy-based casserole. Arrange the vegetables, garlic, herbs and spices on top and fill with cold water to cover. Bring to the boil, reduce to a simmer and place a lid on top. Gently simmer for about 50 minutes to an hour, until the legs are tender and come off the bone easily. Try not to overcook, or the meat will become quite dry.

To make the gremolata, mix the olive oil, garlic, lemon zest and juice and chopped parsley together in a bowl. Season well with salt and pepper to taste.

When ready, remove the rabbit legs to a warm plate and leave to rest for a few minutes. Scoop the vegetables into warmed bowls. Shred the meat of the rabbit legs into large pieces, then divide among the bowls. Pour a ladleful of hot broth over each. Finally, spoon the gremolata over the rabbit legs and vegetables and serve immediately.

Pork fillet stroganoff

This is a lovely, unfussy dish to make for supper. Serve with buttered pasta or fluffy steamed rice.

SERVES 4
500g pork fillet
1 tsp sweet smoked paprika, plus an extra pinch
4 tbsp olive oil
1 onion, finely sliced
2 garlic cloves, finely sliced
200g brown chestnut mushrooms, sliced
splash of brandy
150ml sour cream or double cream
squeeze of lemon juice
handful of flat-leaf parsley, leaves chopped

Trim off any fat or sinew from the pork fillet and slice thinly. Season with salt, pepper and a teaspoon of paprika.

Heat half the olive oil in a wide frying pan until hot. Add the onion and fry over medium heat for 6–8 minutes until soft and translucent, stirring frequently. Add the garlic and mushrooms and increase the heat slightly. Fry for another 3–4 minutes until the mushrooms are tender. Tip the contents of the pan on to a plate and set aside.

Add the remaining oil to the pan and fry the pork fillet over high heat. Fry the meat for 1½–2 minutes until golden brown. Return the onions, garlic and mushrooms to the pan. Add a splash of brandy and let it boil or flambé until almost all reduced. Stir in the cream and bring to a gentle simmer. Adjust the seasoning with a little more salt, pepper and a squeeze of lemon juice. Throw in the chopped parsley and remove the pan from the heat. Serve immediately, sprinkled with a pinch of paprika.

Home-made bangers

I admit, it takes a bit of effort to make your own sausages, but the flavour and texture are superlative. Get the kids to help out and make it fun. For the minced pork, I like to use an equal amount of belly and shoulder or leg meat. As home-made bangers are free from preservatives, they keep for only a few days, so freeze some or eat them as soon as they are made. Serve on a bed of mustard mash with onion gravy or as part of a barbecue.

First, rinse the pork intestines under cold running water for about 5–10 minutes. Hold on well to the slippery things, as they can easily slide down the sinkhole. Soak in a bowl of water with the lemon juice to help remove some of their smell.

Sweat the onion and garlic in olive oil and some seasoning for 6–8 minutes until soft, stirring every now and then. Transfer to a large bowl and leave to cool completely. Mix in the rest of the ingredients. It's probably easiest to use your hands to do this.

Drain the pork intestines and squeeze out any excess water. Pat dry with kitchen paper. If you don't have a sausage-making kit, push the end of a funnel (or a piping bag fitted with a plain round nozzle) through one end of the pork intestines and keep threading the intestine until you've come to the other end, where you tie a knot. Now squeeze or push the filling through the skin, trying not to tear the skin along the way. Keep stuffing until you end up with a long coil. (Get another pair of hands to help with this.) Next, twist 10–12cm lengths of the sausage in alternate directions to get individual sausages. Cut and separate the sausages just before cooking.

Gently fry the sausages in a lightly oiled non-stick pan for 15–20 minutes, turning them occasionally. Use very low heat to ensure that the sausage remains succulent, and do not pierce the skins, as this would only allow the juices to escape. Alternatively, precook them in the oven, then throw them on a hot grill or barbecue to impart a smoky flavour to the bangers (see page 116).

MAKES ABOUT 20

sausage skins/pork intestines, enough to make 20 large sausages
juice of half a lemon
1 large Spanish onion, finely chopped
3 large garlic cloves, finely crushed
2 tbsp olive oil, plus extra to fry the sausages
1kg minced pork
50g fresh breadcrumbs, lightly toasted
large handful of flat-leaf parsley, leaves chopped
handful of lemon thyme, leaves stripped
6 large sage leaves, finely chopped
finely grated zest of 2 lemons
2 tsp fine sea salt
2–3 tsp cracked black peppercorns, to taste
¼ tsp cayenne pepper (optional)

Classic mixed grill

The simplicity of a classic mixed grill makes it perfect for a barbecue. All you need to complete the al fresco meal are a few large bowls of salads on the side.

Heat the oven to 180°C/Gas 4. Put the sausages in a lightly oiled roasting tray and precook in the oven for 15–20 minutes until they are golden and just cooked through, turning them over halfway. Remove and leave to rest for a few minutes.

Prepare the barbecue or heat a griddle pan until hot. First, cook the tomatoes and mushrooms. Place the tomatoes (cut-side up) and the mushrooms (gill-side up) on another lightly oiled baking tray. Drizzle with olive oil and season well with salt and pepper. Cook for 5–7 minutes, turning over halfway, until the tomatoes are just soft and the mushrooms are golden brown. Transfer to a large warm platter and keep warm, preferably in a low oven, or simply covered with a piece of foil.

Barbecue or griddle the bacon rashers and sausages for 2–2½ minutes on each side, turning them occasionally as they cook. Brush the black pudding with a little oil and cook for 2–3 minutes on each side. Remove them all to a large platter and keep warm.

Brush the lamb chops, sirloin steaks and lamb's kidneys with olive oil and season well with salt and pepper. Barbecue or griddle them in batches: the lamb chops will take 1–1½ minutes on each side for medium rare, the sirloin steak needs only 40–50 seconds per side, and the kidney halves will want about a minute on each side. Transfer each batch to another warm platter as they are ready. Allow the meat to rest a little, then bring all the platters to the table and serve.

SERVES 6–8

12 home-made sausages (see page 112)
olive oil, for brushing
12 large tomatoes, halved
12 portabellini (baby portabella) or chestnut mushrooms, cleaned and stalks removed
12 back bacon rashers
750g black pudding, cut into 12 pieces
12 small lamb chops with bone, about 120g each
1.2kg sirloin or rump steaks, cut into 10–12 portions, each about 1cm thick
12 lamb's kidneys, halved
few sprigs of watercress, to garnish

Angus beef olives

These are a reminder of my Scottish roots. When I was young, beef olives were a real treat, even though the stuffing was made with breadcrumbs, herbs and suet. Angus beef sausagemeat is now widely available, and it is perfect for the stuffing, giving this traditional dish a slightly upmarket feel. Serve some mashed potatoes and green beans on the side.

SERVES 4

4 thin slices topside of beef, each about 200g and 1.5cm thick
2 tbsp olive oil
knob of butter
1½ tbsp plain flour
2 tsp tomato purée
150ml dry red wine
300ml beef stock (see page 259)

Stuffing:
2 tbsp olive oil
1 medium onion, finely chopped
1 celery stalk, finely chopped
250g Angus beef sausagemeat (or meat from 4 sausages)
50g fresh breadcrumbs
stripped leaves from a few sprigs of thyme
handful of flat-leaf parsley, chopped
1 large egg, to bind

First, begin the stuffing. Heat the olive oil in a pan and fry the onion and celery for 4–6 minutes, stirring frequently, until soft but not browned. Transfer to a bowl and leave to cool.

Meanwhile, bash the beef slices out between two layers of baking parchment using a meat mallet or a rolling pin. This helps to tenderize the meat, but be careful not to create any splits in the beef.

Once the onion and celery have cooled, mix in the sausagemeat, breadcrumbs, chopped herbs and egg to bind. Mix in a little seasoning. With wet hands, divide the mixture into 4 and roll each portion into a neat oval. Lay a stuffing portion on one end of a flattened beef slice and roll up into a neat log. Tie and secure the log with kitchen string, then wrap with cling film. Holding both ends of the cling film, roll the log on a work surface to even out the shape. Repeat with the remaining beef and stuffing. Chill for at least 30 minutes to allow the beef olives to firm up slightly.

Preheat the oven to 180°C/Gas 4. Heat a thin layer of olive oil in a wide frying pan. Unwrap the beef olives, season lightly and fry until browned all over. Transfer to a large baking dish and return the pan to the heat. Add the butter and flour and stir continuously for a minute, then blend in the tomato purée. Take the pan off the heat and gradually stir in the wine. Return to the heat, pour in the stock and bring to the boil. Stir over high heat until the mixture is smooth and has thickened slightly. Taste and adjust the seasoning.

Pour the sauce over the beef olives and cover the baking dish loosely with a piece of foil. Put the dish in the oven and cook for an hour. Remove the foil and return to the oven for another 30 minutes, turning over halfway, until the beef olives are tender and the sauce has thickened further. Remove the kitchen string, cut into thick slices and serve with the sauce.

Corn-fed chicken legs with braised peas and onions

Mark Sargeant, my head chef at *Claridge's* and general right-hand man, considers this his desert-island dish. The braised peas and onions are similar to 'petits pois à la française', a French classic that even featured on Mark's retro wedding menu, except that then they were served with home-made sausages and mash. As they are the stars of the show, do make sure to use good-quality free-range chicken legs. Battery chickens will not do.

SERVES 4

Chicken legs:
4 large corn-fed chicken legs,
   each about 300–350g
2 tbsp olive oil
small handful of thyme sprigs
1 fat garlic clove, skin on, lightly crushed
20g butter
150ml water

Braised peas and onions:
25g butter
200g baby or pickling onions, peeled
few sprigs of thyme
600g peas, thawed if frozen
150ml water
2 heads of little gem lettuce, shredded

Cut off the knuckles from the chicken legs for a neat presentation and trim off any excess fat. Heat the oil in a large frying pan until hot. Season the chicken legs all over with salt and pepper. Fry for 2 minutes on each side until golden brown. Add the thyme, garlic, butter and water to the pan. Reduce the heat to low, partially cover the pan and braise for 30–40 minutes until the chicken legs are tender. Turn the legs over halfway through cooking.

Fifteen minutes before the chicken legs are ready, melt the butter in another pan and tip in the onions. Toss well and cook over medium-to-low heat for 8–10 minutes, stirring frequently, until the onions are tender. Add the thyme sprigs, peas and water. Season well and simmer for about 5–6 minutes until the peas are tender and the water has mostly cooked off. Add the lettuce and stir for another minute until just wilted.

Spread the braised peas and onions on a large serving platter and arrange the glazed chicken legs on top. Serve immediately.

Goat curry

This is a light, piquant and flavourful curry inspired by the Caribbean goat curries I used to enjoy during the Notting Hill carnival. Here, chicken stock or water take the place of yoghurt or coconut milk (both staples in South Asian and South-east Asian curries), leaving you feeling satisfied but not heavy after the meal. The list of ingredients may seem long, but don't let this daunt you – you most likely have all the vegetables and spices in your kitchen. Serve the goat curry with plain steamed rice and garnish with lots of coriander leaves.

SERVES 4

1kg goat shoulder (or other braising cut)
3 tbsp olive oil
½ tsp turmeric
½ tsp cumin powder or seeds
½ tsp mustard seeds
1 cinnamon stick
2 star anise
4 cardamom pods, lightly crushed
1 tsp soft brown sugar
few curry leaves (optional)
400g tin chopped tomatoes in natural juice

400ml chicken stock (see page 258) or water
handful of coriander leaves, to garnish

Chilli paste:
1 small onion, roughly chopped
4 garlic cloves, peeled
4 small chillies, deseeded and roughly chopped
3cm piece of ginger, roughly chopped
generous pinch of sea salt
3 tbsp groundnut oil

To make the chilli paste, put all the ingredients into a small food processor and whiz to a fine paste. Stop the machine and scrape down the bowl of the processor two or three times to ensure it is all evenly ground. Scrape the paste into a small bowl and set aside.

Cut the goat shoulder into small bite-size chunks and season with salt and pepper. Heat half the oil in a wide saucepan. Fry the meat in two batches until golden brown all over. After each batch, remove to a plate and set aside. Tip the chilli paste into the pan and stir over medium heat for 2–3 minutes until fragrant. Add the dried spices, sugar and curry leaves, if using. Continue to stir for another minute. Add the chopped tomatoes and stock to the pan and stir well. Reduce the heat to the lowest setting. Cover the pan and cook slowly for 3–4 hours until the meat is just tender.

Remove the lid and skim off the excess oil on top. Gently simmer for another 20–30 minutes until the curry has reduced and thickened slightly. The meat should be very tender. Taste and adjust the seasoning, then serve garnished with coriander leaves.

Roast loin of pork with Bramley apple sauce

The secret to a good crackling is to ensure that the pork skin is dry and well-scored. You may struggle to score the skin, as it's tough. I always have a clean, sharp Stanley knife in the kitchen for this sole purpose, but a sharp cook's knife will also do the job. Make sure the oven is very hot when you put the pork in so the skin sizzles quickly.

SERVES 6–8
1.3kg loin of pork
few sprigs of rosemary, leaves chopped
2 large garlic cloves, chopped
finely grated zest of 1 lemon
2 tbsp olive oil
1 onion, sliced
olive oil, to drizzle

Bramley apple sauce:
500g Bramley cooking apples
20g butter
1 tbsp lemon juice
4–5 tbsp caster sugar

Preheat the oven to its highest setting, about 240°C/Gas 9. Remove the butcher's strings if the pork loin is tied. Pat the skin of the pork dry with kitchen paper, then score it in a criss-cross pattern at 2cm increments. Turn the pork loin over so that the flesh side is upwards. Cut a slit along the thick side of the loin, without cutting all the way through, to open it out like a book.

Mix the chopped rosemary, garlic, lemon zest, olive oil and a generous pinch each of salt and pepper in a small bowl. Stir well, then spread the mixture over the pork loin. Sprinkle with a little more salt and pepper. Roll up the loin and secure tightly with kitchen string in 3–4cm increments. Rub the scored skin with a large pinch of salt.

Scatter the sliced onions on a roasting tray and put the pork on top, with the skin facing upwards. Drizzle the skin generously with olive oil and sprinkle over another large pinch of salt. Transfer the baking tray to the hot oven and roast for 20 minutes until the skin is golden and starting to crisp.

Turn down the oven to 180°C/Gas 4 and roast for another 30–40 minutes or until the pork is just cooked through. To test, insert a metal skewer into the thickest part of the loin and press gently: the juices should be clear. (I prefer to serve my pork just slightly pink to retain its succulence and moisture.) Rest for 10–15 minutes before carving.

Make the apple sauce while the pork is roasting. Peel, quarter and core the apples. Roughly chop into quarters, then put in a medium saucepan with the butter, lemon juice, 4 tablespoons of sugar and a splash of water. Cover the pan and cook over low heat for about 15 minutes. Lift the lid and give the apples a stir every now and then, adding a little more water if the pan looks too dry. When they have broken down into a purée, taste for sweetness and add a little more sugar to taste. Adjust the consistency with a little more hot water as necessary. Serve warm with the roast pork.

Sweet potato and duck rösti with fried duck eggs

Sweet potato with tender duck meat is a fabulous combination, and the soft, runny yolks of duck eggs bring the dish together. Serve this with a sharply dressed salad on the side to contrast with the sweetness and richness of the main dish.

Scrape off the fat from the duck legs and peel off the skin. Pull the meat off the bones and shred into small pieces. Place in a large bowl. Peel and coarsely grate the sweet potatoes over the bowl. Add the egg whites, cornflour and a pinch each of salt and pepper and mix well.

Heat a drizzle of olive oil in a wide non-stick pan. Spoon 3–4 neat piles of rösti mixture on the pan and press down to flatten them and form thin patties. Fry over low-to-medium heat for about 4–5 minutes until golden brown. Flip over and cook the other side for the same amount of time. Transfer to a plate lined with kitchen paper and keep warm. Repeat with the remaining rösti mixture. You may find that you won't need additional oil after the first batch.

While the last batch of rösti is cooking, heat a little oil in another frying pan (or several blini pans). Fry the duck eggs for 1–2 minutes until the egg whites are set but the yolk is still runny in the middle.

Stack 2 potato and duck rösti on each of 4 warm serving plates and top each with a fried duck egg. Serve immediately.

SERVES 4
2 confit duck legs (sold in jars or tins), each about 150g
2 medium sweet potatoes, about 225g
2 large egg whites
1 tbsp cornflour
little olive oil, for cooking
4 fresh duck eggs

Honey roast ham

A large glazed ham need not be confined to Christmas dinner – make it the next time you have a big gathering of family or friends. You probably need to order the ham in advance from a good butcher. (Illustrated on page 129.)

(Illustrated on page 129.)

SERVES 8–10
half a leg of unsmoked gammon with bone, about 4.5kg, soaked overnight
1 large carrot, halved
1 large onion, quartered
2 celery stalks, cut into large chunks
1 bay leaf
few sprigs of thyme
1 tsp black peppercorns
about 50 cloves, to stud

For the glaze:
100ml honey
100g demerara sugar
50ml Madeira wine
3 tbsp soy sauce
3 tbsp English mustard
2 tbsp Worcestershire sauce

Cumberland sauce:
3cm piece of ginger, finely grated
3 tbsp port
5 tbsp redcurrant jelly
150g fresh cranberries
small pinch of cayenne pepper
finely grated zest of 1 large orange, plus juice of half
finely grated zest of 1 lemon
1 stem ginger in syrup, finely sliced into matchsticks

Find a pan large enough to fit the gammon and put it inside. Add the carrot, onion and celery, and fill with cold water to cover. Bring to the boil, then turn down the heat to a simmer. Scoop off any scum that rises to the surface of the liquid. Add the bay leaf, thyme and peppercorns. Simmer for 3–4 hours, topping up the water level with boiling water as necessary. The gammon is ready when the meat comes away from the bone easily.

Meanwhile, prepare the glaze. Put the honey and demerara sugar in a saucepan and bring to the boil, stirring until the sugar has dissolved. When the mixture begins to foam, remove the pan from the heat and carefully pour in the Madeira. The sugar will spit and splatter, so take care not to burn your hands. If the sugar hardens, return the pan to the heat and stir until it dissolves again. Leave to cool slightly, then stir in the remaining ingredients. Cool completely.

Lift out the ham to a large roasting tin and leave to cool slightly. (Save the stock to make soup if it is not too salty.) Preheat the oven to 170°C/Gas 3. Cut away the skin of the ham, leaving behind an even layer of fat. Score the fat all over in a criss-cross pattern, then stud with cloves, pressing each into the middle of a scored diamond.

Brush the glaze over the ham and bake for about an hour, basting frequently with the glaze. When nicely browned, remove from the oven and leave to rest for 15 minutes before carving.

For the Cumberland sauce, put the ginger, port, redcurrant jelly, cranberries, cayenne pepper and orange juice into a saucepan and bring to a simmer. Cook for 5–10 minutes until thickened and syrupy. Take the pan off the heat and stir in the lemon and orange zests and stem ginger. Transfer to a serving bowl and leave to go cold. Serve with thin slices of honey roast ham.

Cider and honey roast leg of lamb

Apples and cider go wonderfully with lamb. The apples break down on cooking and help thicken the sauce. Crisp roast potatoes and steamed tender stem broccoli make the perfect accompaniments.

SERVES 6

1 leg of lamb, about 2kg, fat trimmed and skin scored
olive oil, to drizzle
3–4 garlic cloves, skins on and halved
few sprigs of thyme
juice from half a lemon
4 apples, russets or braeburns
500ml medium cider
runny honey, to drizzle
300ml lamb or chicken stock (see page 262 or 258)

Preheat the oven to 220°C/Gas 7. Weigh the lamb and calculate the final cooking time at 12 minutes per 450g for medium rare, 15 minutes per 450g for medium. Score the fat around the leg of lamb in a criss-cross pattern, drizzle with a little olive oil, then rub all over with salt and pepper. Place in a deep roasting pan and scatter the garlic and thyme over and around. Pour over the lemon juice and drizzle again with olive oil. Sprinkle with a little more seasoning, then roast in the hot oven for 20 minutes.

Slice the apples into quarters and cut off the cores. Remove the lamb from the oven and reduce the heat to 180°C/Gas 4. Scatter the apples around the pan and baste the lamb with the cider. Turn the lamb over and drizzle with 2 tablespoons of honey. Return to the oven for 30 minutes.

Turn the lamb round, baste the meat with the pan juices, then drizzle over another tablespoon of honey. Continue to roast for the calculated time. To check, insert a skewer into the thickest part of the lamb, then press the meat lightly: the redder the juices, the rarer the meat. Lift the lamb to a carving board and cover with a piece of foil. Rest in a warm place while you prepare the gravy.

At this point, the apples and garlic in the roasting pan should be very soft. Press with a fork, then tip the entire contents of the pan into a fine sieve over a saucepan. Push down with the back of a ladle to extract all the juices and flavour from the apples and garlic. Discard the pulp. Place the saucepan over medium heat and add the stock. Bring to the boil and let it bubble vigorously until the sauce has thickened to a desired gravy consistency. Taste and adjust the seasoning, then pour into a warm serving jug. Carve the lamb into thin slices and serve drizzled with the apple and cider gravy.

Lamb shank cassoulet

This is my posh version of the classic French cassoulet, which was traditionally a layered casserole made with breast of lamb, salted pork, haricot beans and Toulouse sausages. I'm using lamb shanks because I adore their fantastic flavour and texture. This recipe will satisfy four very hungry football players, or you could pull the meat off the shanks and serve the dish quite adequately to six. Serve with sautéed savoy cabbage and chunks of country bread on the side.

SERVES 4–6
4 lamb shanks, each about 350g
3 tbsp olive oil
50g smoked back bacon, fat trimmed, chopped
2 large Spanish onions, thinly sliced
3 garlic cloves, chopped
2 tbsp tomato purée
few sprigs of thyme
2 bay leaves
250ml dry white wine
1 litre lamb or chicken stock (see page 262 or 258)
2 x 400g tins haricot beans, rinsed and drained
4–6 Toulouse sausages

To serve:
30g butter
75g fresh breadcrumbs
stripped leaves from a sprig of thyme

Season the lamb shanks with salt and pepper. Heat a cast-iron or heavy-based pan with a thin layer of oil. Fry the lamb over medium heat for about 2 minutes on each side until evenly browned all over. Transfer to a large plate and set aside.

Add another tablespoon of oil to the pan and stir in the bacon. Fry for a few minutes until the bacon is golden brown. Add the onions and garlic and stir well. Cover the pan and sweat the onions for 4–6 minutes until they are translucent.

Remove the lid and add the tomato purée and herbs. Stir for a couple of minutes, then pour in the white wine. Let the wine boil until it has reduced by two-thirds. Pour in the stock and bring to a simmer. Return the lamb to the pan and put a crumpled piece of baking parchment on top. This will prevent any meat that pokes out of the liquid from drying out. Turn the heat to the lowest setting and gently simmer for 2½–3 hours, turning the lamb shanks over halfway, until they are tender and will come away from the bone easily.

Remove the shanks to a warm platter, cover with a piece of foil and leave to rest. Skim off the excess fat from the surface of the braising liquid, then boil until reduced by more than half. Lower the heat, add the beans and sausages to the pan and simmer for about 10 minutes until the sausages are cooked through. Taste and adjust the seasoning. If necessary, return the lamb shanks to the pan to reheat for a few minutes.

Melt the butter in a frying pan and tip in the breadcrumbs, thyme leaves and a little salt and pepper. Stir over medium heat until the breadcrumbs are golden and crisp. Remove the pan from the heat.

Divide the lamb shanks among warm plates and spoon the beans, sausages and sauce around them. Sprinkle over the crispy breadcrumbs and serve immediately.

Roast rib-eye with caramelized shallot and red wine gravy

An ideal roast for Sunday lunch. As with any roast, a great end result depends as much on the quality of the meat as the cooking. Spend a little more on a good joint and you're halfway there. If you buy a rib-eye with the bone in, choose one that weighs 2 to 2.5 kilograms for this dish. Good with mashed potatoes and steamed broccoli.

Preheat the oven to 230°C/Gas 8. Drizzle the beef with a little olive oil, then rub all over with salt, pepper and the chopped rosemary. Put the beef on a bed of rosemary sprigs in a large roasting tin so that the fat is on top. Roast in the hot oven for 20 minutes, then reduce the heat to 190°C/Gas 5. Roast for 12 minutes per 450g for medium rare or 18 minutes per 450g if you prefer it medium. Turn the beef halfway through cooking for an even roast. To check if the beef is cooked, insert a thin skewer and press lightly: the pinker the juice, the rarer the meat.

Remove the beef from the oven, transfer to a warm platter and loosely cover with a piece of foil. Leave to rest for 15–20 minutes while you make the gravy.

Remove the rosemary sprigs, then pour off the excess fat from the roasting tin, leaving behind a couple of tablespoons. Place the tin over medium heat. Add the shallots, garlic and a little salt and pepper. Fry for about 5–6 minutes, stirring frequently, until the shallots begin to soften. Increase the heat slightly and fry until the shallots are golden and lightly caramelized. Add the flour and stir for a few more minutes. Pour in the vinegar and red wine and stir well to mix. Pour in the stock and bring to the boil. Boil for about 10–15 minutes until the sauce has reduced and thickened to your liking. Season well to taste, then stir in the tarragon.

Carve the beef thinly and serve the gravy in a warm jug.

SERVES 6–8
1.5–2kg beef rib-eye, trimmed
2 tbsp olive oil
large handful of rosemary, leaves of a few sprigs chopped

Gravy:
2 banana shallots, thinly sliced
1 garlic clove, crushed
2 tbsp plain flour
1–2 tbsp balsamic vinegar
150ml red wine
500ml beef stock (see page 259)
few sprigs of tarragon, leaves chopped

Lamb stew with bacon, sweet onions and prunes

I love the combination of flavours in this stew – sweet onions and prunes offset salty, smoky bacon to create a sweet and savoury sauce for tender lamb. If you have some in the larder, stir a couple of tablespoons of quince paste to the stew to give it another dimension of flavour and sweetness. The stew is delicious served with creamy, buttery polenta or butternut squash purée.

SERVES 4–6

1 medium boned leg of lamb (about 650g)
2–3 tbsp olive oil
250g smoked bacon or pancetta, chopped
1 large Spanish onion, finely sliced
100g silverskin or pickling onions,
   rinsed and drained
1½ tsp caster sugar

generous splash of dry white wine
1 cinnamon stick
1 tsp ground ginger
2 tbsp quince paste or membrillo (optional)
125g soft pitted prunes, halved
500ml lamb stock (see page 262)

Trim off the fat and sinew from the leg of lamb and cut it into small chunks. Season with salt and pepper. Heat a thin layer of olive oil in a heavy-based pan or a cast-iron casserole until hot. Fry the lamb in several batches to avoid overcrowding the pan. The pieces should take about 2 minutes to brown on each side. As they are ready, remove to a plate and set aside.

Add a little more oil to the pan and fry the chopped bacon for 3–4 minutes until lightly browned. Tip in the Spanish and silverskin onions and stir frequently over medium heat. Cook for 4–6 minutes until the onions begin to soften. Add the sugar and a little more salt and pepper and cook for another 2–3 minutes until the onions have slightly caramelized. Deglaze the pan with a generous splash of white wine, scraping the bottom of the pan with a wooden spoon to dislodge the sediment. Let the wine boil down until reduced to a sticky glaze.

Return the meat to the pan and stir in the cinnamon, ginger, quince paste (if using) and half the prunes. Pour in the stock and bring it to a gentle simmer. Cover the pan and turn the heat down to low. Cook, stirring occasionally, for an hour. Add the remaining prunes to the pan and cook for another 30 minutes until the lamb is very tender. Taste and adjust the seasoning before serving.

Braised chicken legs with honey and five-spice

This is a delicious and unusual chicken dish. I like to serve it with parsnip mash and wilted spring greens on the side. You could also make this with duck – a good way to introduce children to the meat.

Trim off the excess fat around the chicken legs and set aside. Put the Szechuan peppercorns in a dry roasting pan and toss over high heat for 1–2 minutes until fragrant. Tip in to a mortar and add the five-spice powder and a generous pinch each of salt and pepper. Lightly grind the mixture with a pestle, then use to sprinkle all over the chicken legs.

Heat a deep-sided sauté pan with a little olive oil. Add the chicken legs and turn the heat down to medium. Cook for 3–4 minutes on each side until the legs are evenly browned. Remove them to a plate and set aside.

Add the onions and ginger to the pan with a little more oil, if needed. Cook, stirring occasionally, for 6–7 minutes until the onions are soft. Add the honey and white wine. Simmer until the pan is quite dry and the wine and honey have reduced to a sticky glaze. Pour in the chicken stock and return to a simmer.

Return the chicken legs to the pan and braise for another 40–45 minutes, turning them over halfway, until tender. If you prefer the sauce to be thicker, add the cornflour mixture and simmer for a couple of minutes until thickened. Serve immediately on warm plates.

SERVES 4

4 free-range chicken legs
1 tsp Szechuan peppercorns
1 tsp Chinese five-spice powder
1–2 tbsp olive oil
2 medium onions, finely sliced
1 tbsp finely grated ginger
2 tbsp runny honey
splash of dry white wine
400ml chicken stock (see page 258)
1 tsp cornflour mixed with 1 tbsp water (optional)

Duck breasts with port and cherry sauce

Duck and cherries are a classic pairing. Use fresh English cherries in the summer or a jar of preserved cherries in kirsch at other times of the year.

SERVES 4

4 Gressingham duck breasts, each about 200–225g, with skins on
1 banana (or 3 regular) shallot, finely chopped
200ml port
250g cherries, pitted
2 tbsp black cherry conserve or jam
300ml chicken stock (see page 258)
½ tsp cornflour or arrowroot mixed with few tbsp water (optional)

Braised bok choy:
15g knob of butter
8 medium heads of bok choy (each about 70g), halved lengthways

Season the duck breasts with salt and pepper and place, skin-side down, on a dry frying pan. (You don't need to add any oil to the pan, as the duck skins are very fatty.) Place the pan over gentle heat for 8–10 minutes until most of the fat has been rendered. Increase the heat slightly and fry until the skins are golden brown. Flip the breasts and cook the other side for another 3–4 minutes until the meat feels slightly springy and the duck is cooked to medium rare. Remove to a warm plate and leave to rest.

Pour off most of the fat from the pan. (Save for roasting potatoes.) Add the shallot and stir over medium-to-low heat for 4–5 minutes until soft. Increase the heat and pour in the port to deglaze. Boil until the port has reduced right down and the pan is quite dry. Add the cherries, black cherry conserve and chicken stock. Return to the boil and boil until reduced by more than half and the sauce is syrupy. If you prefer the sauce thicker, add the cornflour mixture and boil for a few minutes more.

When you are about ready to serve, put a glassful of water, the butter and some seasoning into a sauté pan over high heat. As soon as the butter has melted, add the bok choy and braise for 2 minutes until just wilted, turning them over halfway. Drain on a large plate lined with kitchen paper.

Divide the bok choy and duck breasts among warm serving plates and spoon over the port and cherry sauce. Serve immediately.

pies
and tarts

My mother, even as a working woman with four children, would bake a few pies or tarts every Friday night. We'd have them for supper and there'd still be leftovers for tea on Sunday. I adored my mum's shepherd's pie, and it's still one of my favourite dishes to this day. I order it with a side of courgettes every time Tana and I go to *The Ivy*. They make it amazingly well – add a few dashes of Worcestershire sauce, and I'm in heaven!

To me, pies and tarts represent casual, relaxed cooking, and I wish more people still had the time or inclination to make them. As well as being enjoyed at suppers and picnics, pies and tarts can be elevated to fine dining. At our restaurant in Paris, we serve an amazing cannon of lamb with a side dish neatly filled with a small serving of shepherd's pie. Everyone loves it, and it made me proud to present our version of a British classic to our French guests.

Raised game pie
Shepherd's pie with Branston pickle
Cornish chicken pie
Smoked salmon and horseradish cream tartlets
Fish pie with oysters and scallops
Spinach, feta and pine nut tart
Crab and tarragon tart
Artichoke, asparagus and ham quiche
Lemon, leek and dolcelatte tart
Wild mushroom tart with parmesan and walnut pastry

Raised game pie

An old-fashioned raised game pie is perfect sustenance for a day out hunting or mushroom-picking. I've made individual pies, but you could also make a large one to share. This may need another 10–15 minutes in the oven. Whichever you choose, plan ahead, as the finished pies need to set overnight. (Illustrated on page 147.)

MAKES 4 INDIVIDUAL PIES

Hot-water crust pastry:
250g plain flour
½ tsp fine sea salt
1 large egg
50g unsalted butter
50g lard
85ml water

Pie filling:
250g loin of venison
150g partridge, pheasant or guinea fowl breasts
2 rashers of smoked back bacon, about 50g, fat trimmed, chopped
200g pork or venison sausagemeat
1 tbsp each freshly chopped parsley and sage
grated zest of 1 lemon
5 juniper berries, finely ground with a pinch of sea salt
2 egg yolks, lightly beaten with 1 tbsp water, for egg wash

To serve:
pickled onions (see page 192)
piccalilli (see page 193)

Begin by making the pastry. Sift the flour and salt into a mixing bowl and make a well in the middle. Crack the egg into the well and sprinkle over some of the flour to cover. Put the butter, lard and water in a small pan and heat gently. Once the butter and lard has melted, increase the heat and bring to the boil.

Pour the boiling water and fat round the edge of the bowl and quickly stir together using a butter knife. Knead the dough lightly until smooth. It will be quite soft at this stage. Wrap in cling film and chill for at least an hour until the pastry is firm.

Meanwhile, prepare the filling. Trim the game meat of any fat or sinew, then cut into 2cm cubes. Mix with the bacon, sausagemeat, herbs, lemon zest and crushed juniper berries and season with salt and pepper. Divide the mixture into 4 equal portions and roll into balls.

Cut out one-third of the pastry for making the pie lids. Wrap it in cling film and chill. Roll the remaining pastry out on a lightly floured work surface to about the thickness of a £1 coin. Use a saucer of about 14cm in diameter as a template to cut out 4 circles. Roll the reserved pastry to the same thickness, and from this cut out round lids large enough to fit each pie: about 7cm in diameter.

Place a stuffing ball in the middle of each pastry base and place a lid on top. Brush the border of the pastry base with the egg wash, then mould it up and round the filling to meet the lid. Curl the edge of the lid up to meet the top inside edge of the pie case and pinch together to seal. Repeat with the others, then crimp the edges to decorate. Chill until the pastry feels firm.

Preheat the oven to 190°C/Gas 5. Make a neat steam hole in the centre of each pie lid with a small knife. Bake the pies for 15 minutes. Remove them from the oven and brush evenly with the remaining egg wash. Reduce the oven temperature to 170°C/Gas 3 and bake for a further 20–30 minutes until the pastry is cooked and the centre of the pie is hot. To test, insert a metal skewer into the centre of the pies for a few seconds, then feel it against your hand or lip. It should feel hot to the touch. Allow the pies to cool on a wire rack. Serve cold with pickled onions and piccalilli.

Shepherd's pie with Branston pickle

A traditional shepherd's pie with a little bit of chopped Branston pickle to enhance the flavour of the lamb mince. As with cottage pie, this freezes well. Add another 10–15 minutes to the cooking time if cooking from frozen.

SERVES 4

500g lean minced lamb
2–3 tbsp olive oil
1 large onion, finely chopped
1 large carrot, finely chopped
2 garlic cloves, chopped
2 tbsp plain flour
1 tbsp tomato purée
250ml red wine
350ml chicken stock (see page 258)
1½ tbsp worcestershire sauce
leaves from a handful of thyme sprigs
leaves from a sprig of rosemary, chopped
2½ tbsp finely chopped Branston pickle

Potato topping:
600g desirée potatoes, cut into chunks
50g butter
30ml hot milk
3 tbsp freshly grated parmesan
2 large egg yolks

Put a wide cast-iron or other heavy-based pan over moderate-to-high heat. Season the lamb mince with salt and pepper and fry in a thin layer of oil for about 10 minutes until evenly browned. (Fry the mince in 2 batches if your pan is not wide enough to brown it in one go.) Transfer the mince to a bowl using a slotted spoon.

Add a little more olive oil to the pan and stir in the onion, carrot and garlic. Fry for another 4–5 minutes, stirring frequently, until the vegetables are golden brown. Add the flour and tomato purée and stir frequently for another couple of minutes. Pour in the red wine and scrape the bottom of the pan to dislodge the browned sediment. Let the wine boil until it has almost all reduced and the pan is quite dry.

Pour in the chicken stock and bring to a simmer. Return the mince to the pan and add the Worcestershire sauce and herbs. Turn the heat to the lowest setting and partially cover the pan. Simmer for 30–40 minutes, stirring every once in a while, until the lamb is tender and the sauce has thickened.

Meanwhile, boil the potatoes in salted water for 15–20 minutes until tender when pierced with a small knife. Drain well, then return to the hot pan over low heat to dry out briefly. Press them through a potato ricer into a large bowl. Mix in the butter, hot milk and 2 tablespoons of parmesan. Season well to taste, then beat in the egg yolks and set aside.

Preheat the oven to 180°C/Gas 4. Fold the chopped Branston pickle through the mince mixture and spoon into a 2-litre ovenproof dish. Using a large spoon, layer the mashed potato generously on top of the mince, starting from the outside and working your way into the middle. Fluff up the mashed potato with a fork to make rough peaks. Sprinkle over the remaining parmesan and grate over a little black pepper. Bake for approximately 20–25 minutes until the topping is golden brown and the sauce is bubbling round the sides. Serve with extra Branston pickle on the side if you wish.

Cornish chicken pie

No other food makes me quite as enjoyably nostalgic as a good home-made chicken pie. When we were young, my mother used to make a mean chicken pie from scratch – pastry, chicken stock and everything – with whatever little time or resources she had. Here is my version of this ultimate British comfort food. (Illustrated on page 151.)

SERVES 4
800ml chicken stock (see page 258)
leaves from a sprig of thyme
3 large skinless boneless chicken breasts, about 600g
300g baby onions or small shallots, peeled
200g button mushrooms, cleaned
50g butter
50g plain flour
100ml double cream
500g shortcrust pastry (see page 263)
2 large egg yolks, lightly beaten with 1 tbsp water, for egg wash
coarse sea salt, to sprinkle

Bring the stock to a simmer in a medium saucepan. Add the thyme leaves, then poach the chicken breasts for 10–12 minutes until just firm and cooked through. With a pair of kitchen tongs, transfer the poached chicken to a plate and leave to cool.

Tip the baby onions into the stock and simmer for 5 minutes. Add the mushrooms and cook for another 4–5 minutes until both the onions and mushrooms are tender. Using a slotted spoon, transfer the onions and mushrooms to a large bowl.

Increase the heat under the stock and boil until reduced to 300ml. Meanwhile, cut the chicken into bite-size pieces and add to the onions and mushrooms. When the stock has reduced, pour it into a jug.

Return the pan to the heat. Melt the butter and stir in the flour. Keep stirring over medium heat for 3–4 minutes. Gradually pour in the hot stock, stirring continuously, until fully incorporated and the sauce is smooth. Simmer for 5–10 minutes until thickened, then stir in the cream and return to a simmer. Season to taste with salt and pepper. The sauce should be thick and creamy. Pour over the chicken and vegetables and mix well. Leave to cool completely.

Preheat the oven to 200°C/Gas 6. Divide the pastry into 2: two-thirds in 1 portion and one-third in the other. Roll out the larger portion on a lightly floured surface to a circle large enough to cover a 23–25cm-wide, 3–4cm-deep pie tin. Line the pie tin and trim off the excess pastry. For the good-looking result, put a blackbird or pie funnel in the middle of the tin. Spread the filling evenly over the base.

Roll out the remaining pastry to form a lid for the pie and cut a cross in the middle to fit round the blackbird. (If you're not using a pie funnel, cut a small cross anyway, to serve as a steam vent.) Brush the pastry rim with the egg wash, then drape the pastry lid over the pie and press down round the rim to seal. Use a sharp knife to cut off any excess pastry round the rim, then crimp the edges. If you wish, decorate the pie with pastry leaves made with the trimmings. Brush the pie top and trimmings with the egg wash, sprinkle the top with coarse sea salt, then bake for about 35 minutes until the pastry is golden brown and the sauce is bubbling from the steam hole.

Smoked salmon and horseradish cream tartlets

These tarts make a perfect starter for a dinner party. To get ahead, bake the tartlet shells 2–3 days in advance and store in an airtight container to keep them crisp. (I rarely make my own puff pastry. I buy it instead, but from a good source, of course, such as Dorset Pastry.) The smoked salmon filling can also be prepared beforehand, but bear in mind that the flavour of the raw shallots will become stronger with time. Serve with dressed salad leaves on the side.

SERVES 4

250g ready-made puff pastry
200g hot-smoked salmon
1 large shallot, finely chopped
half a celery stalk, very finely chopped
2 tbsp horseradish cream
6 tbsp crème fraiche
pinch of cayenne pepper
squeeze of lemon juice
small handful of dill, leaves chopped, plus few fronds to garnish
4 large slices of smoked salmon, to garnish

Begin by making the tartlet cases. Cut the pastry into 4 portions, then roll out each one on a floured surface to about the thickness of a £1 coin. Prick all over with a fork, then use them to line four 10cm tartlet tins with removable bases. Let the pastry protrude a little above the sides of the tin. Use a pair of kitchen scissors to trim away bigger pieces of excess pastry because they are vulnerable to breaking off. Carefully stack the pastry-lined tins, one on top of the other, pushing the tins down to keep the shape of the pastry. Chill for 30 minutes.

Preheat the oven to 200°C/Gas 6. Put the stacked pastry cases on a baking sheet, then line the uppermost pastry with foil and baking beans. Bake for 25–30 minutes until golden brown. Remove the foil and beans and carefully separate the tartlet tins. Place them on the baking sheet and return to the oven for another 5–10 minutes until golden and cooked through. Remove from the oven and leave the pastries to cool in the tins. Use a sharp knife to trim off the excess pastry level with the rims.

Put the hot-smoked salmon, shallot and celery in a food processor and blend until smooth. Add the horseradish and crème fraiche and pulse for a few more seconds until they become incorporated into the mixture. Season to taste with salt, pepper, cayenne pepper and lemon juice. Fold in the chopped dill. Transfer to a bowl and chill for at least an hour to let the mixture set a little and allow the flavours to come together.

Remove the tartlet cases from the tins and spread with the filling. Drape the smoked salmon slices attractively over the filling and garnish the tarts with a few dill fronds.

Fish pie with oysters and scallops

The scallops lend sweetness to the pie, while fresh oysters help to enrich and season the filling with their natural salt. Buttered spinach is a good side dish for this.

First, prepare the sauce for the filling. Heat the butter in a pan and sweat the shallots until soft. Add the wine and Noilly Prat and reduce by half. Add the stock and bubble away again until reduced by half. Pour in the cream and boil until reduced to a thick sauce consistency. Strain through a sieve and discard the shallot. Stir in the mustard, if using, and check for seasoning, adding a little lemon juice to taste. Leave to cool completely.

Next, make the mash topping. Put the potatoes into a pan of salted water and bring to the boil. Cook for 15–20 minutes until tender when pierced with a knife. Drain well and push them through a potato ricer. Mix in the butter and hot milk until melted and well incorporated. Season to taste and leave to cool slightly. Beat the egg yolks lightly, then mix into the cooled mash. Set aside while you prepare the fish.

Heat the oven to 180°C/Gas 4. Check the fish fillets for any small bones, removing any with tweezers, then cut into 3cm chunks. Season lightly, then gently fold the fish, oysters and scallops into the sauce with the basil leaves. Transfer to a 1.75–2-litre ovenproof baking dish. Spread the mash over the filling and run a fork over it for a rustic finish. Grate over a layer of parmesan. Bake for about 25–35 minutes until the pie is bubbling and golden brown on top.

SERVES 4–6
Fish filling:
800g firm fish fillets, such as salmon and/or monkfish
6 oysters, shucked
6 large scallops, cut in half
handful of basil leaves

Sauce:
20g butter
2 shallots, finely chopped
75ml dry white wine
75ml Noilly Prat
150ml fish stock (see page 262)
150ml double cream
1 tbsp dijon mustard (optional)
squeeze of lemon juice

Mash topping:
3 large desirée potatoes, about 750g, cut into large chunks
75g butter, cut into cubes
50ml hot milk
2 large egg yolks
parmesan, for grating

Spinach, feta and pine nut tart

This tart is based on the Greek spanakopita. As I've never been a huge fan of filo pastry, my version uses shortcrust.

SERVES 4

300g shortcrust pastry (see page 263)
2 tbsp olive oil
2 sweet onions (such as vidalia),
   finely chopped
500g spinach leaves, washed and drained
nutmeg, to grate

250g feta cheese, crumbled
1 large egg
1 large egg yolk
200ml double cream
50g toasted pine nuts
4 tbsp freshly grated parmesan

Roll out the pastry on a lightly floured surface to about the thickness of a £1 coin, then use it to line a 23–25cm tart tin, 3–4cm deep, with a removable base. Press the pastry into the edges of the tin and leave a little excess overhanging the sides. Chill for at least 30 minutes.

Meanwhile, prepare the filling. Heat the olive oil in a pan and fry the onions with a little salt and pepper. Stir frequently over medium heat until soft but not browned: about 6–8 minutes. Wilt the spinach leaves in a large pan in several batches. Stir them over medium-to-high heat just until they've wilted, then transfer to a colander set over a large bowl. Press down on the spinach with the back of a ladle to squeeze out the excess water, cool slightly, then roughly chop into smaller pieces.

Put the onion and spinach in a large bowl and grate over a little nutmeg. Add the feta, egg, egg yolk, cream and a generous grating of black pepper. Add a pinch of salt to taste, bearing in mind that the feta is already salty. Finally, fold in the pine nuts and 3 tablespoons of the parmesan. Chill until ready to use.

Heat the oven to 200°C/Gas 6. Line the pastry with foil and fill with baking beans. Bake blind for 15–20 minutes until the sides are lightly golden. Remove the foil and beans and return to the oven for another 5 minutes until the base is golden and there are no uncooked patches left. Remove from the oven and reduce the oven temperature to 170°C/Gas 3. Use a sharp knife to trim off the overhanging pastry, then set aside to cool.

Spread the filling evenly over the pastry shell, then sprinkle with the remaining parmesan. Bake for about 35–40 minutes until the top is golden brown and the filling has set. Cool slightly before unmoulding, slicing and serving.

Crab and tarragon tart

This tart is light but, at the same time, indulgent. I advise against using tinned crabmeat because the excess brine in it will dilute the custard and make the pastry soggy. Fresh crabmeat is greatly superior in taste, too.

Roll out the pastry on a lightly floured surface to about the thickness of a £1 coin, then use it to line a 23–25cm tart tin, 3–4cm deep, with a removable base. Press the pastry into the edges of the tin and leave a little excess overhanging the sides. Chill for at least 30 minutes.

Preheat the oven to 200°C/Gas 6. Line the pastry with foil and fill with baking beans. Bake blind for 15–20 minutes until the sides are lightly golden. Remove the foil and beans and return to the oven for another 5 minutes until the base is golden and there are no uncooked patches left. Take the pastry out of the oven and cool slightly. Using a sharp knife, trim off the excess pastry level with the rim.

Reduce the oven temperature to 180°C/Gas 4. Pick through the crabmeat and discard any pieces of shell or cartilage. In a large mixing bowl, lightly beat together the crème fraiche, sour cream, mustard, parmesan and lemon juice and zest. Stir in the crabmeat and tarragon, then season well with salt and pepper to taste. Lightly beat the eggs and stir into the mixture.

Bake the tart for about 35–40 minutes until it is puffed and golden on top but slightly wobbly in the centre. Remove the tart from the oven and let it cool a little before slicing and serving.

SERVES 6 AS A STARTER OR 4 AS A LIGHT LUNCH
300g shortcrust pastry (see page 263)
450g white crabmeat
200ml crème fraiche
100ml sour cream
1 tbsp wholegrain mustard
2 tbsp freshly grated parmesan
zest and juice of 1 small lemon
small bunch of tarragon, leaves finely chopped
2 large eggs

Artichoke, asparagus and ham quiche

This is a wonderful quiche to make when local asparagus is in season or when you have leftover glazed ham (see page 130) after a Sunday lunch. (Illustrated on page 161.)

SERVES 4–6
300g shortcrust pastry (see page 263)
300g bunch of asparagus
3 large eggs
250ml crème fraiche
85g gruyère, grated
150g cooked ham, cut into cubes
290g artichoke hearts in olive oil, drained weight 220g, halved or quartered

Roll out the pastry on a lightly floured surface to about the thickness of a £1 coin, then use it to line a 23–25cm tart tin, 3–4cm deep, with a removable base. Press the pastry into the edges of the tin and leave a little excess overhanging the sides. Chill for at least 30 minutes.

Meanwhile, trim the ends of the asparagus and peel the tough stalks. Cut them into finger lengths, then blanch in a pan of salted water for about 3 minutes until just tender and bright green. Drain and refresh in a bowl of iced water, then drain again.

Preheat the oven to 200°C/Gas 6. Line the pastry with foil and fill with baking beans. Bake blind for 15–20 minutes until the sides are lightly golden. Remove the foil and beans and return to the oven for another 5 minutes until the base is golden and there are no uncooked patches left. Take the pastry out of the oven and cool slightly. Using a sharp knife, trim off the excess pastry level with the rim.

For the filling, beat together the eggs and crème fraiche with a pinch each of salt and pepper. Stir in three-quarters of the gruyère. Evenly scatter the cooked ham, artichoke hearts and asparagus around the pastry base. Spoon over the filling to come just below the rim. You may not need all the filling. Sprinkle the remaining cheese on top and bake in the bottom third of the oven for about 30–35 minutes until the filling is set and golden on top. Cool slightly, then unmould and slice. Eat warm or at room temperature.

Lemon, leek and dolcelatte tart

This is a free-form tart – ideal for those who cannot be bothered to line pie tins, blind-bake the pastry and wash up the tins afterwards. As it is filled and baked in one go, the base of the pastry will not be as crisp as one that has been blind-baked. If you are making the pastry yourself, add the finely grated zest of a small lemon for extra zing.

Remove the outer leaves of the leeks, trim off the ends and slice finely. Melt the butter in a large pan over medium heat. As it begins to foam, add the leeks, thyme and some salt and pepper. Cover the pan and cook for 8–10 minutes until the leeks are soft but not coloured. Lift the lid and give the leeks a stir every once in a while. Remove the lid and stir over high heat to cook off any excess moisture in the leeks and dry them out. Transfer to a mixing bowl and leave to cool.

Preheat the oven to 200°C/Gas 6 and leave a large baking sheet inside. Roll out the pastry on a lightly floured work surface to about the thickness of a £1 coin. Use a 25cm round dinner plate as a guide to cut out a neat circle from the pastry. Transfer the pastry, draping it over the rolling pin, on to another baking sheet.

Mix the crème fraiche, parmesan, lemon zest and juice and three-quarters of the dolcelatte with the leeks. Season to taste, then stir in the egg.

Spread the leek and cheese filling evenly over the pastry, leaving a 2.5cm border, then crumble over the remaining dolcelatte. Fold the pastry border over the filling and carefully crimp the edges. Brush the crimped edges with the egg wash.

Put the tart and baking sheet on to the hot sheet in the oven. Bake for 20 minutes, then reduce the temperature to 180°C/Gas 4 and cook for another 15–20 minutes until the pastry is golden brown. Leave to cool for 5 minutes before slicing and serving.

SERVES 4

4 large leeks, about 1kg, washed
25g butter
leaves from a few sprigs of thyme
300g shortcrust pastry (see page 263)
150ml crème fraiche
3 tbsp freshly grated parmesan
zest of 1 lemon
1 tbsp lemon juice
100g dolcelatte, crumbled
1 large egg, lightly beaten
1 medium egg yolk, lightly beaten with 1 tbsp water, for egg wash

Wild mushroom tart with parmesan and walnut pastry

The flavours in this tart are earthy and rich. When wild mushrooms are in season, I use a combination of ceps, chanterelles, pieds de bleu, pieds de mouton, trompettes de la mort, mousserons and girolles. At other times of year, a mixture of sliced portabellas and chestnut mushrooms does the job.

Roll out the pastry on a lightly floured surface to about the thickness of a £1 coin, then use it to line a 23–25cm tart tin, 3–4cm deep, with a removable base. Press the pastry into the edges of the tin and leave a little excess overhanging the sides. Chill for at least 30 minutes.

Preheat the oven to 190°C/Gas 5. Line the pastry with foil and fill with baking beans. Bake blind for 15–20 minutes until the sides are lightly golden. Remove the foil and beans and return to the oven for another 5 minutes until the base is golden and there are no uncooked patches left. Remove from the oven and reduce the oven temperature to 170°C/Gas 3. Use a sharp knife to trim off the overhanging pastry, then set aside to cool.

Meanwhile, prepare the filling. Melt the butter in a wide frying pan and add the shallots. Sauté the shallots for 3–4 minutes until they begin to soften. Add the thyme leaves, mushrooms and some salt and pepper. Fry the mushrooms over high heat for 4–5 minutes until any moisture they release has been cooked off. Transfer to a bowl and leave to cool.

For the custard, whisk together the crème fraiche, double cream, egg and egg yolk, salt and pepper in a medium bowl. Once cooled, spread the mushrooms evenly in the tart shell and pour over the custard. Bake the tart for 35–45 minutes until the custard is golden and slightly puffed. Remove from the oven and leave to cool for a few minutes before unmoulding. Slice and serve warm or at room temperature.

SERVES 4–6

300g walnut and parmesan
  pastry (see page 263)
25g unsalted butter
2 shallots, finely chopped
leaves from a few sprigs
  of thyme
350g mixed fresh wild
  mushrooms, large ones
  sliced
200ml crème fraiche
150ml double cream
1 large egg
1 large egg yolk
½ tsp fine sea salt
½ tsp freshly ground
  black pepper

vegetables
and salads

I've included a selection of vegetable dishes and salads using seasonal ingredients in this chapter. Even as a young lad, I understood the importance and joy of eating locally grown fruits and vegetables. My dad moved us around a lot, and there was a time when we lived near Evesham. There I used to spend school holidays cutting asparagus or picking potatoes for pocket money. Lunch was usually a simple soup made with vegetable trimmings, but it tasted of the garden because the ingredients were super-fresh. When the season gets into full swing, taste a home-grown asparagus spear alongside an imported one, and you'll know what I mean.

Walnut, celery, chicory and apple salad
Roast winter vegetables
Glazed Brussels sprouts with chestnuts and pancetta
Roasted tomatoes with marjoram
Spicy cauliflower stir-fry
Braised celery hearts with bacon
Caramelized fennel and red onions
Artichokes braised with onions and lardons
Chicory, goat's cheese and strawberry salad with pine nuts
New potato, pea and broad bean salad with mustard dressing
Grilled aubergines with balsamic, feta and mint
Mixed mushroom salad
Braised red cabbage with Bramley apple
Pickled onions
Home-made piccalilli

Walnut, celery, chicory and apple salad

This is a simple, modern take on the classic Waldorf salad. To make it a main course, add slices of cold smoked chicken or leftover roast chicken or turkey.

First, prepare the dressing by combining all the ingredients in a bowl and seasoning with black pepper to taste.

Trim off the bases of the chicory and separate the leaves. Scatter a few leaves over each serving plate. Trim and roughly chop the celery and include any leaves, then place in a bowl. Core and thinly slice the apples, add to the celery and toss with a little lemon juice to prevent them from discolouring. Add half the walnuts and toss well. Divide among the serving plates and scatter the remaining walnuts over the top. Either drizzle the dressing over the salad or serve in individual dipping bowls on the side.

SERVES 4
2 heads of chicory
4 celery stalks
2 medium apples
squeeze of lemon juice
handful of toasted walnut halves, chopped

Dressing:
3 tbsp mayonnaise (see page 258)
2 tbsp natural or Greek yoghurt
½ tsp celery salt
1 tbsp lemon juice

Roast winter vegetables

I'm a big fan of humble root vegetables, particularly the less attractive ones that tend to be overlooked in the vegetable aisle, such as celeriac, swede and kohlrabi. Each vegetable has a distinctive flavour that is intensified when roasted. An obvious pairing with any roast meat, this dish can also be converted into a vegetarian main course with the addition of some robust salad leaves: drizzle with a creamy yoghurt dressing and then finish off with a sprinkling of soft goat's cheese.

SERVES 4–6
half a large swede
half a large turnip
half a large celeriac
1 kohlrabi (optional)
2 large carrots
2 large parsnips
olive oil, to drizzle
few sprigs of thyme and rosemary, leaves stripped
runny honey, to drizzle (optional)

Heat the oven to 200°C/Gas 6 and leave 1 large or 2 medium roasting trays inside. Peel the swede, turnip, celeriac and kohlrabi, if using, and then cut them into 2cm-thick chunks. Peel the carrots and parsnips and cut into halves or quarters lengthways, similar to the thickness of the other root vegetables.

Put all the vegetables in a large bowl and drizzle with a little olive oil. Sprinkle with salt, pepper and the herbs. Toss well to coat. Remove the tray (or trays) from the oven and spread the vegetables in an even layer. Roast for 25–30 minutes until the vegetables are golden brown and tender, turning them halfway.

If you wish, toss the vegetables with a light drizzle of honey to glaze. Tip into a warm serving platter and bring to the table.

Glazed Brussels sprouts with chestnuts and pancetta

I think it's pretty safe to say that in most households, Brussels sprouts are cooked only once a year as part of the Christmas menu. It is such a shame, for when cooked properly, these nutritious little cabbages are delicious, especially when matched with cured bacon (or pancetta) and chestnuts. For extra flavour, sprinkle on some finely grated parmesan and a few toasted almond flakes.

Trim off a little of the base from the Brussels sprouts while you bring a pan of salted water to the boil. You do not need to mark a cross at the bottom of the sprouts – all this does is allow them to become waterlogged during cooking.

Blanch the sprouts for 8–10 minutes until they are just tender but still retain a bite. Drain, refresh in a bowl of iced water until cooled, then drain again. Cut the sprouts in half so that they will take in more flavour from the other ingredients.

Just before you are ready to serve, heat the oil and butter in a pan and fry the pancetta until golden brown and crisp. Tip in the chestnuts, chilli flakes and thyme leaves and stir over medium-to-high heat to warm the chestnuts. Add the blanched sprouts and a splash of water. Stir-fry for a minute or 2 until the sprouts are warmed through and the liquid has cooked off. Season generously with black pepper, then transfer to a warm platter and serve.

SERVES 4
500g Brussels sprouts
2 tbsp olive oil
knob of butter
4 slices of pancetta, chopped
200g chestnuts, roughly chopped
small pinch of chilli flakes
leaves from a sprig of thyme

Roasted tomatoes with marjoram

Roasting tomatoes intensifies their flavour, and they make an appetizing addition to salads, pasta dishes or as accompaniments to fish, poultry or meat.

SERVES 4
800g vine-ripened plum tomatoes
2 large garlic cloves, thinly sliced
leaves from a handful of fresh marjoram
3–4 tbsp olive oil

Heat the oven to 150°C/Gas 2. Halve the tomatoes lengthways and then place cut-side up in a shallow baking dish, making sure they are well spaced. Place a slice of garlic on each tomato half, then scatter over the marjoram leaves. Drizzle over a little olive oil and sprinkle with a pinch of salt and pepper.

Bake for 30 minutes, basting the tomatoes with pan juices halfway through cooking. Serve warm or at room temperature.

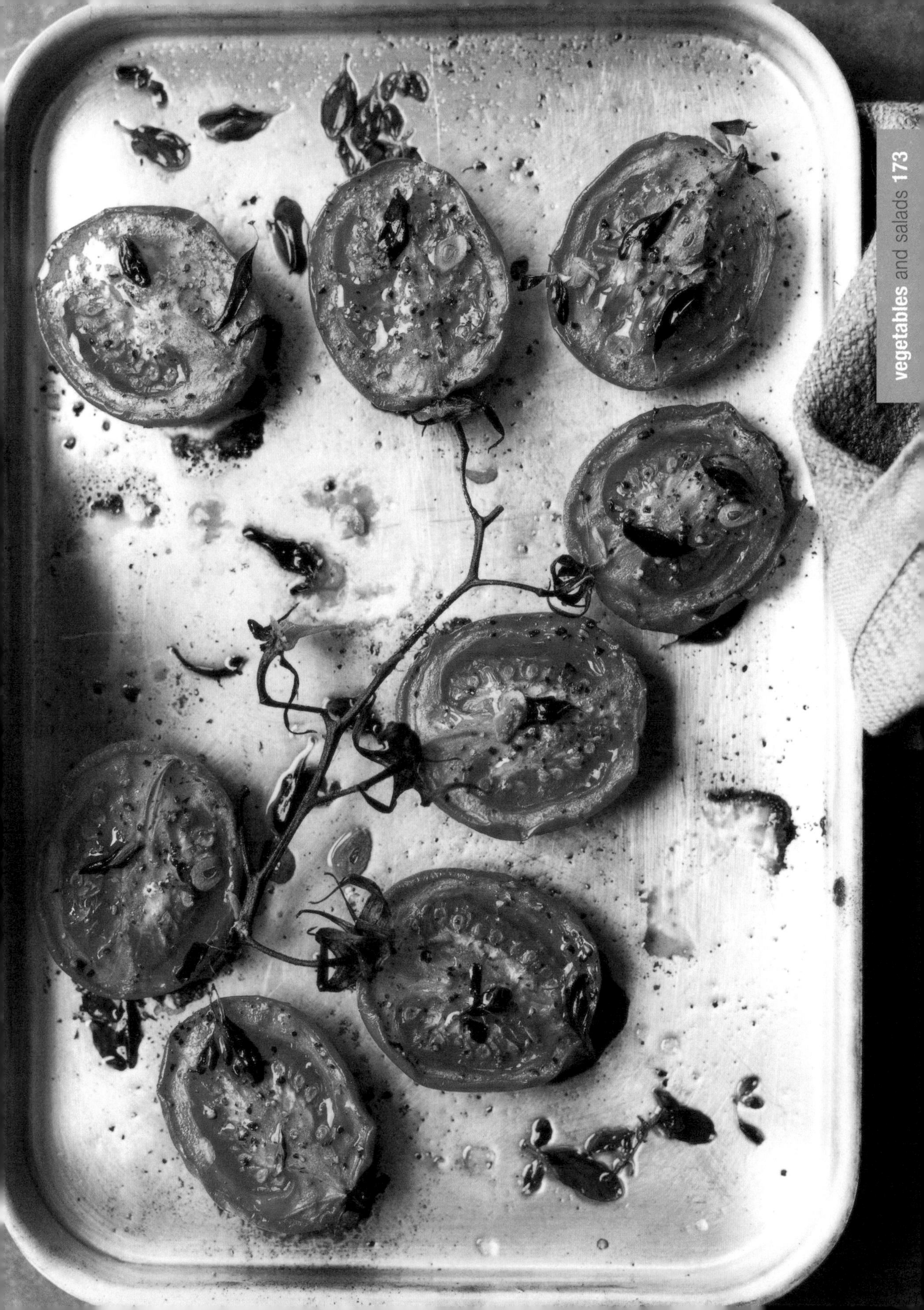

Spicy cauliflower stir-fry

Fragrant and warm Indian spices can really improve the flavour of the relatively bland cauliflower. This goes to explain why many recipes for cauliflower soup include a dash of curry powder. This dish makes a wonderful accompaniment to an Indian meal, and I also like to serve it with fried fish.

SERVES 4

1 medium cauliflower, about 550g
½ tsp fenugreek
½ tsp coriander seeds
½ tsp cumin seeds
⅛ tsp ground turmeric
2 tbsp olive oil
1 large onion, finely sliced
3 garlic cloves, finely chopped
1 large red chilli, deseeded and finely chopped
100ml vegetable or chicken stock (see pages 258–9)

Cut the cauliflower into small florets and set aside. Lightly toast the fenugreek, coriander and cumin seeds in a dry pan for a couple of minutes until fragrant. Tip into a mortar and add the ground turmeric and a pinch of salt and pepper. Grind to a fine powder.

Heat the oil in a large pan or a wok. Add the onions and a little salt and pepper. Stir over low heat for about 6 minutes until the onions are soft but not browned. Add the garlic, chilli and ground spices and stir-fry for another minute.

Add the cauliflower florets and pour over the stock. Cook for 6–8 minutes, stirring frequently, until the cauliflower is just tender and most of the stock has been absorbed or cooked off. Taste and adjust the seasoning and serve warm.

Braised celery hearts with bacon

Tender and flavourful braised celery hearts are especially good with pork and chicken. For a simple week-night supper, serve with poached chicken breasts and steamed rice or creamy polenta.

If using whole heads of celery, cut 15–20cm off the top half and reserve to use in soups or salads. Remove the tough outer ribs until you reach the tender, light yellowish-green hearts. Quarter the hearts lengthways.

Heat the oil in a sauté pan over medium heat. Add the bacon and fry for 4–5 minutes until golden round the edges, then add the garlic and fry for another minute. Add the oregano, stock and tomato purée to the pan and stir well to mix. Add the celery hearts and gently simmer for 20–30 minutes, partially covered, until tender when pierced with a skewer. Transfer the celery and any sauce in the pan to a platter and serve warm.

SERVES 4–6

- **4–6 celery hearts or whole heads of celery**
- **2 tbsp olive oil**
- **3 rashers of smoked back bacon, chopped into lardons**
- **2 large garlic cloves, finely sliced**
- **¼ tsp dried oregano**
- **300ml chicken or vegetable stock (see pages 258–9)**
- **2 tbsp tomato purée**

Caramelized fennel and red onions

Fennel and onions have similar qualities: both become tender, sweet and mellow when cooked, and caramelizing them helps to bring out their natural sugars. This easy side dish is ideal with roast pork or chicken.

Trim off the bases of the fennel bulbs and cut them lengthways into thick wedges. Peel and cut the onions into quarters. Set aside. Tip the fennel seeds into a mortar with a generous pinch of salt and pepper. Grind to a powder and sprinkle over the onions and fennel.

Heat a wide sauté pan with the olive oil until hot. In batches, fry the onions and fennel over high heat until golden brown. They should take about 2–3 minutes on each side. Return all the browned onion and fennel to the pan, pour in the wine and stock and dot with a few knobs of butter. Cover with a dampened piece of crumpled greaseproof paper. Cover with a lid and bring to the boil, then reduce the heat and simmer until nearly all of the wine has been absorbed: about 30–40 minutes. Transfer to a warm platter to serve.

SERVES 4
2 large fennel bulbs
4 large red (or white) onions
½ tsp fennel seeds
2 tbsp olive oil
100ml dry white wine
100ml chicken or vegetable stock (see pages 258–9)
few knobs of butter

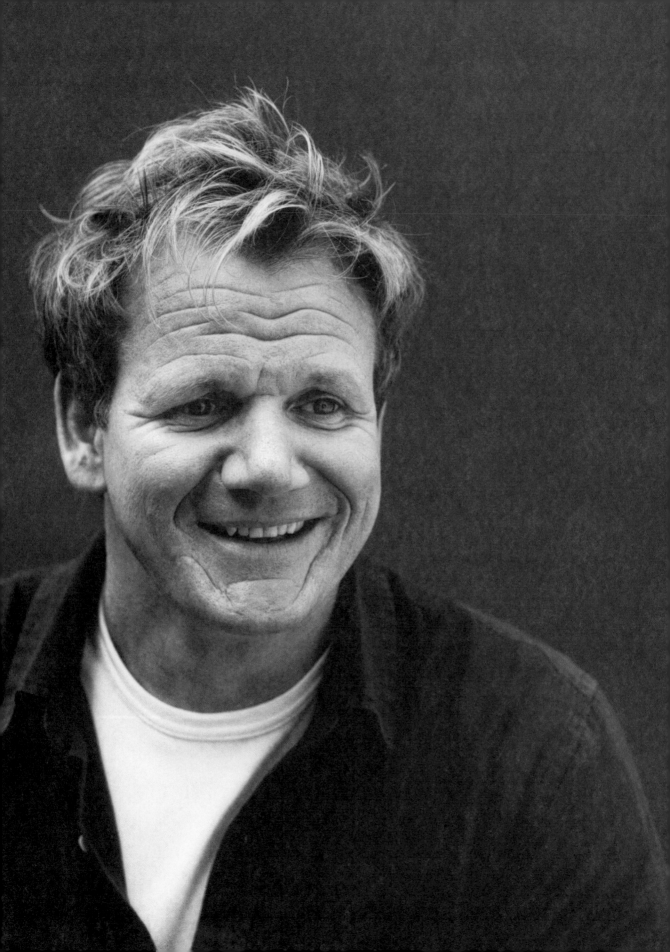

Artichokes braised with onions and lardons

This dish is based on artichoke barigoule, a classic provençale dish in which artichokes are gently poached in fragrant stock, which is then boiled down to make a sauce. Perfect with any white or oily fish. (Illustrated on page 180.)

Fill a large bowl with water and squeeze the lemon halves into it. Working with one artichoke at a time, cut in half crossways. Discard the top and pull off the outer green leaves until you reach the tender yellow leaves. If the artichoke is old, scrape out the hairy choke with a melon baller or spoon. Trim and peel the base and stem, then quarter the heart. Add to the bowl of lemon water and repeat with the remaining artichokes.

Heat 2 tablespoons of olive oil in a medium pan. Drain the artichokes and pat dry with a clean tea towel. In batches, fry the artichokes, cut-side down, until the edges are golden brown. Remove to a plate and set aside.

Add the bacon to the pan, with a little more oil as necessary, and sauté for 4–5 minutes until slightly browned. Add the onion and stir occasionally for 4–6 minutes until the onion is transparent. Add the garlic, thyme, basil stems and coriander seeds, then deglaze the pan with the wine. Boil until reduced by two-thirds, then pour in the chicken stock. Return to the boil and simmer until reduced by half.

Return the artichokes to the pan. Simmer for 8–10 minutes, turning the artichokes over halfway, until they are tender. Remove the artichokes and most of the onions and lardons to a plate, then boil the sauce until reduced to a syrupy glaze. Return the artichokes and onions and lardons to the pan and toss to coat in the sauce.

Adjust the seasoning and transfer the vegetables to a warm bowl. Tear the basil leaves and scatter over the artichokes to serve.

SERVES 4
1 lemon, halved
8 medium-sized artichokes
2–3 tbsp olive oil
1 rasher of smoked bacon, chopped into lardons
1 small onion, chopped
3 garlic cloves, thinly sliced
few sprigs of thyme
few sprigs of basil, stalks and leaves separated
½ tsp coriander seeds
75ml dry white wine
400ml chicken stock (see page 258)

Chicory, goat's cheese and strawberry salad with pine nuts

This fresh and colourful salad says summer to me. I've also made it with raspberries, tumbling a handful over each plate and thickening the dressing with a few crushed berries.

SERVES 4–5
2 heads of chicory
100g wild rocket
150g strawberries, hulled and quartered
50g toasted pine nuts
200g soft goat's cheese

Dressing:
1 tbsp red wine vinegar
3 tbsp raspberry vinegar
100ml extra virgin olive oil
pinch of caster sugar

Trim off the base of the chicory and pull apart the leaves. Add to a salad bowl with the rocket leaves and toss lightly. Scatter over the strawberries and pine nuts, then crumble over the goat's cheese. Just before serving, whisk together all the ingredients for the dressing (or put them into a screwtop bottle and shake well), seasoning to taste, and drizzle over the salad; you may not need all of it. Toss the salad and serve.

New potato, pea and broad bean salad with mustard dressing

Waxy potatoes are best for this salad. My favourites are the slightly nutty charlotte potatoes, but small red-skinned potatoes or anya potatoes also work well. If you need to save time, cook the broad beans a little longer and leave them in their skins.

Boil the potatoes in a pan of salted water for 10–15 minutes until tender when pierced with a skewer. Meanwhile, whisk together all the ingredients for the dressing (or put them into a screw-top bottle and shake well).

Bring another pot of salted water to the boil. Blanch the peas and broad beans separately for 3 minutes until tender. Drain, refresh in a bowl of iced water and drain again. Squeeze out the broad beans and discard the pale skins.

When cooked, drain the potatoes in a colander and leave to cool slightly. If you wish, peel off the skins using a small knife and wearing gloves to protect your hands. Put the potatoes into a large bowl and, while still warm, toss with the dressing to coat. Stir in the peas and broad beans. Taste and adjust the seasoning. Garnish with a few dill sprigs and serve.

SERVES 4–6
750g evenly sized new
**   potatoes, washed**
100g peas (thawed,
**   if frozen)**
150g podded broad beans
few sprigs of dill, to garnish

Mustard dressing:
4 tbsp extra virgin olive oil
1 tbsp white wine vinegar
1½ tsp dijon mustard
1½ tsp wholegrain mustard
handful of tarragon and dill,
**   chopped**
pinch of sugar (optional)

Grilled aubergines with balsamic, feta and mint

Although you can easily grill the aubergines using a griddle pan, I prefer to cook them over a barbecue, where they take on a lovely smoky quality. However, if the weather is uncooperative (as it is most times of the year), add a little sweet paprika to the olive oil and brush over the aubergine slices to give them a smoky flavour.

Preheat the barbecue or place a griddle pan over high heat. Trim and thinly slice the aubergines. Mix the olive oil with the chopped garlic and some seasoning in a small bowl. Brush the oil on both sides of the aubergine slices, then cook them for about 2 minutes each side until tender.

Overlap the grilled aubergine slices on a platter and scatter over the cherry tomatoes and feta cheese. Drizzle over a little balsamic vinegar and finish off with a generous grating of black pepper and a sprinkling of chopped mint.

SERVES 4–5
2 medium aubergines
50ml olive oil, plus extra
  to drizzle
1 fat garlic clove, finely
  chopped
75g cherry tomatoes, halved
100–125g feta cheese,
  crumbled
good-quality aged balsamic
  vinegar, to drizzle
small handful of mint,
  leaves chopped

Mixed mushroom salad

The earthy flavour of wild mushrooms is unbeatable. When they are not in season, use a mixture of shiitake, oyster, portabella and/or brown chestnut mushrooms.

SERVES 4
2 shallots, thinly sliced
1½ tbsp olive oil, plus extra to drizzle
30g butter
600g mixed mushrooms, such as portabella, ceps, girolles and chestnut, thinly sliced
squeeze of lemon juice
1–2 tbsp walnut oil
large handful of flat-leaf parsley, leaves roughly chopped
100g rocket or mixed salad leaves

Place a wide frying pan over medium heat. Sauté the shallots with the olive oil for about 4–6 minutes until soft. Add the butter to melt and as it begins to foam, add the mushrooms and some salt and pepper. Toss over high heat for 2–3 minutes until the mushrooms are lightly browned and any liquid released has been cooked off.

Tip the sautéed mushrooms and shallots into a bowl. Squeeze over a little lemon juice and drizzle over the walnut oil. Add the chopped parsley and season again to taste.

Just before serving, toss the rocket or salad leaves with a little lemon juice and olive oil, then place neat piles on each serving plate. Divide the mushrooms among the plates and serve.

Braised red cabbage with Bramley apple

This gorgeous braised cabbage, which features again and again on our restaurant menus, is a fantastic accompaniment to game or other rich red meat. It keeps well in the refrigerator for about a week. (Illustrated on page 191.)

Preheat the oven to 180°C/Gas 4. Quarter, core and finely shred the cabbage. Peel, core and thickly slice the apple. Set aside.

Put the butter, sugar and vinegar in an ovenproof pan and stir over medium heat until the sugar has dissolved. Add the cinnamon, cloves and a generous pinch of salt and pepper. Tip in the cabbage and apple and toss well to coat. Put a wet, crumpled piece of greaseproof paper on top and transfer the pan to the oven.

Bake for 1½ hours until tender. Carefully lift the greaseproof paper and give the mixture a stir every half an hour, dampening the paper each time to prevent it from burning. Remove the greaseproof paper and bake for a final 15–20 minutes, stirring halfway, until the cabbage is tender and the liquid in the pan has reduced to a syrupy glaze.

SERVES 4
1 small red cabbage, about 600g
1 large Bramley apple
150g butter
150g light brown sugar
150ml cider vinegar or clear malt vinegar
2 cinnamon sticks
¼ tsp ground cloves

Pickled onions

There's nothing quite like home-made pickled onions! Remember to use preserving jars with non-metal lids, as the pickling vinegar will rust metal. (Illustrated alongside the pie on page 147.)

MAKES ABOUT 500G
200g coarse salt
500ml water
500g pickling onions or baby shallots
750ml malt vinegar
250ml cider vinegar
2 tsp each of coriander seeds, mustard seeds, allspice, black peppercorns and mace
2 bay leaves
25g root ginger, bruised
1 tbsp caster sugar

First, make a brine. Put the salt and water in a saucepan and stir over low heat until fully dissolved. Pour into a large bowl and leave to cool completely.

Meanwhile, peel the onions or shallots. (It may be easier to remove the skins if you quickly blanch the onions in boiling water for 30 seconds, refresh in cold water and then drain well.) Add the peeled onions to the brine, then place a plate on top to submerge them in the liquid. Leave to soak in a cool part of the kitchen for 24 hours.

Put the vinegars, dried spices, bay leaves and ginger into a non-reactive pan (such as stainless steel, enamel or non-stick) with the sugar. Boil for 20–25 minutes, then strain the vinegar through a fine sieve and discard the spice. Leave to cool completely.

Rinse the onions and drain well. Divide them between the sterilized jars, pour over the pickling liquid to cover and seal the jars tightly. Leave the onions to pickle in a cool, dark place for at least 2 weeks, preferably a month, before eating. Refrigerate after opening.

Home-made piccalilli

Piccalilli is the ultimate accompaniment to a raised game pie (see page 144 for recipe and page 147 for illustration) or cold meat terrine. If you can't find fresh pickling onions, use small shallots or the tiny pink Thai ones you can get in specialist grocery stores.

Dissolve the salt in about a litre of warm water in a large stockpot. Add the onions and cauliflower to the pot and place a plate on top to keep the vegetables submerged in the brine. Leave to soak in a cool part of the kitchen overnight. The next day, drain the vegetables and rinse under a cold running tap. Drain well.

Dissolve the sugar in the vinegar over a low heat, then boil for 15–20 minutes until reduced by half. Add 300ml water, then return to the boil. Mix the cornflour and mustard powder together, then stir in several tablespoons of the reduced vinegar to make a smooth paste. Whisk this back into the rest of the vinegar.

Heat the oil in a large saucepan and gently fry the ginger and turmeric for 1–2 minutes. Lower the heat, then gradually add the reduced vinegar mixture, stirring continuously as you pour. Bring the mixture to a simmer and cook for 2–3 minutes until it starts to thicken and coats the back of your spoon.

Add the vegetables to the pan, bring to the boil and simmer for 3 minutes until the cauliflower has softened and the onions are cooked through but retain a bite. Add a little salt and pepper to taste. Spoon into sterilized jars and seal while still warm. Store in a dark, cool place for one month before eating. The flavour improves the longer you keep the piccalilli.

MAKES ABOUT 1.5 LITRES
50g fine sea salt
500g pearl onions or small pickling onions, peeled
1 small cauliflower, about 500g, cut into small florets
150g caster sugar
600ml cider vinegar
2 tbsp cornflour
2 tbsp dry English mustard powder
2 tbsp olive oil
1½ tbsp ground ginger
1½ tbsp ground turmeric

puddings
and ices

Nostalgia is a powerful emotion when it comes to food. Or perhaps I should say that food is a powerful evoker of nostalgia. My work takes me around the world to countries with fascinating and delicious cuisines, but as soon as I reach home, I develop a craving for old-fashioned British puddings.

That traditional puddings are enjoying a revival is clear from the success of my pub menus. Apple pies, rice puddings and lemon meringue pies always sell out. In many cases, we've updated classic recipes, adding a little stem ginger to fruit crumbles and using luscious and creamy lemon tarts as the base for lemon meringue pies. Some recipes, however, I prefer unmodified: my mother's Bakewell tart, for example.

Pear and frangipane tart
Autumn fruit salad with thyme and ginger
Strawberry and champagne granita
Caramelized apple pie
Summer berry trifle
Peach, raspberry and ginger crumble
Baked gooseberries with honey and almonds
Fig ice cream
Cinnamon rice pudding with apricot compote
Custard tart
Lemon meringue pie
Bakewell tart
Poached rhubarb with ginger ice cream
Mixed berry tartlets with vanilla and peach cream
Blackberry sorbet with shortbread fingers

Pear and frangipane tart

This beautiful and delicious tart is – by a piece of good fortune – quick and easy to make. What could be better? It can be served warm or at room temperature, and is ideal fodder for a lavish picnic. (Illustrated on page 198.)

(Illustrated on page 198.)

SERVES 4–6

Tart:
300g ready-made puff pastry (see introductory note on page 154)
1 egg yolk, beaten with 2 tsp water, to glaze
2 large or 3 medium ripe pears

Sugar syrup:
50g caster sugar
50ml water
1 cinnamon stick
2 star anise
juice of 1 lemon

Frangipane:
75g butter, softened to room temperature
75g icing sugar, plus extra for dusting
1 medium egg, lightly beaten
75g ground almonds
2 tbsp plain flour
1½ tsp Amaretto

Roll out the pastry on a lightly floured surface to about the thickness of a £1 coin, and use a 20cm round cake tin as a guide to cut out a neat circle. Transfer the pastry to a baking sheet, then lightly score a 1.5–2cm edge round it. Brush the rim with the egg wash to glaze, then chill while you prepare the filling.

Place all the ingredients for the sugar syrup in a small saucepan and stir over low heat until the sugar has dissolved. Increase the heat and simmer for 10 minutes until thickened slightly, then leave to cool.

Meanwhile, beat together the butter and sugar for the frangipane. Slowly add the egg, mixing until fully incorporated. Add the almonds and flour and fold through. Finally, mix in the Amaretto. Let the mixture stand for 5 minutes.

Peel the pears, then cut each in half lengthways. Remove the cores with a small spoon or a melon baller and discard. Cut each pear lengthways into thin slices, place in a large bowl and pour over the cooled sugar syrup. Leave them to macerate for a few minutes while you preheat the oven to 190ºC/Gas 5, using the conventional setting. (It is best not to use a fan oven for this recipe.)

Spread a layer of frangipane evenly over the pastry round, leaving the glazed rim clear. Drain the pears, dab dry with kitchen paper, then arrange on top in a concentric circle. Sift over a little icing sugar. Bake until the pears are tender and the filling is golden brown and set: about 35–45 minutes. Remove the tart from the oven and leave to cool slightly. If you like, brush over the pears with the remaining syrup.

Autumn fruit salad with thyme and ginger

Serve this as a light and healthy dessert or as part of a breakfast spread. Put out a large bowl of yoghurt to serve alongside if you wish.

SERVES 4
3–4 ripe plums
1 red apple
1 green apple
2 ripe pears

Thyme and ginger syrup:
1 vanilla pod, split lengthways and seeds scraped
1 star anise
½ tsp coriander seeds
few sprigs of thyme
3cm fresh ginger, peeled and sliced
100g caster sugar
100ml water

Begin by making the thyme and ginger syrup. Put all the ingredients in a pan and stir over low heat until the sugar has dissolved. Increase the heat to a simmer and cook for about 10 minutes until the syrup has thickened slightly.

Meanwhile, cut the plums in half and remove the seeds. Quarter and remove the cores from the apples and pears. Place all the fruit in a large bowl. While the syrup is still piping hot, pour it over the fruit and toss well to coat. Leave to cool, then chill for at least 30 minutes before serving.

Strawberry and champagne granita

A sophisticated and refreshing dessert for hot days. To make it child-friendly, use cranberry juice in place of champagne and top with a little cold milk to make a milky strawberry slush. Stick a wide straw into each glass to complete the deal. The granita will also serve well as a refreshing palate-cleanser between courses.

Hull and roughly chop the strawberries, then put them into a large heatproof bowl. Stir in the sugar and water, then stand the bowl over a pan of gently simmering water. Stir the strawberries frequently to help dissolve the sugar. Carefully cover the bowl with a plate (or the lid of a saucepan) and gently steam for about 30–40 minutes until the strawberries are very soft and have released their juices.

Remove the bowl from the heat and strain the strawberry juice through a fine sieve into a clean bowl. Cool, then mix in the champagne and lemon juice. Pour the mixture into a wide, shallow container and freeze for 1–2 hours until partially frozen. Stir the ice crystals round the sides of the container into the liquid centre. Return to the freezer for another couple of hours and give the mixture another stir.

When ready to serve, hull and cut a few strawberries into quarters. Drop them into individual serving glasses. Scrape the granita with a strong spoon and place into the glasses over the strawberries. If you wish, pour in a splash of champagne and serve immediately.

SERVES 4–6
900g ripe strawberries, plus handful to garnish
125g caster sugar
3 tbsp water
150ml champagne, plus optional extra to serve
2 tbsp lemon juice

Caramelized apple pie

I love the flavour of caramelized apples in a tarte tatin, and this is a way of bringing that flavour into a classic apple pie. Also, because the apples are precooked, they won't shrink during baking and create air pockets inside the pie. I like to serve the pie while it's still warm, with either a little pouring cream or a scoop of vanilla ice cream.

Start by preparing the caramelized apple filling. Mix the sugar, cinnamon and nutmeg together in a bowl. Peel, quarter and core the apples, then cut into thick chunks. Place in a bowl and sprinkle with the spiced sugar to coat. Fry the apples in 2 batches. Melt half the butter in a wide non-stick frying pan and add half the apple chunks. Fry over high heat for about 5 minutes until golden and caramelized round the edges, then transfer to a large bowl and repeat with the remaining apples and butter. Leave to cool completely.

Preheat the oven to 190°C/Gas 5. Roll out the pastry on a lightly floured surface to about the thickness of a £1 coin. Overturn a 20cm pie dish on top of the pastry and cut out a rough circle slightly bigger than the dish. Line the dish with the pastry circle, lightly pressing down to remove any air pockets, then trim off the excess pastry. Re-roll the pastry trimmings into another circle, again slightly wider than the dish, to form a lid for the pie.

Spoon the cooled apples evenly over the lined pie dish. Brush the pastry rim with a little water, then use a rolling pin to drape the pastry lid over the pie. Press down lightly to seal, then trim off the excess pastry. (If you wish, use excess pastry to decorate the pie.) Crimp the edges and brush over with the egg wash to glaze. Use the tip of a knife to cut a small cross in the centre so that steam can escape during cooking. Sprinkle over a little caster sugar.

Bake for 35–40 minutes until the crust is golden brown and crisp. Let stand for 15–20 minutes before serving.

SERVES 8
90g caster sugar
½ tsp ground cinnamon
pinch of freshly grated nutmeg
4 large Bramley apples, about 1.5kg
60g unsalted butter
500g sweet flan pastry (see page 263)
1 large egg yolk, beaten with 2 tsp water, to glaze

Summer berry trifle

These pretty little trifles appeal to any age group – it all depends on what style of serving glass you use. The only specification I give is that the glasses be crystal clear, so as to show off the red berries against the cool and pale layers of creamy custard. To add a little crunch, sprinkle the filled glasses with lightly crushed amaretti biscuits before you top with the remaining fruit.

SERVES 8

Custard:
600ml whole milk
1 vanilla pod, split lengthways
   and seeds scraped
85g caster sugar
6 large egg yolks
40g cornflour
150ml double cream

Trifle:
150g raspberries
150g strawberries
150g redcurrants
1 tbsp crème de cassis
1 tbsp icing sugar, or to taste

Put the milk, vanilla pod and seeds, and a tablespoon of the sugar into a saucepan and bring to a simmer. Meanwhile, beat the egg yolks, cornflour and remaining sugar together in a bowl. Slowly pour in the hot milk, stirring all the time to prevent the eggs from scrambling. When fully incorporated, rinse out the pan. Strain the mixture back into the clean pan and return to the heat. Whisk over low heat until it thickens sufficiently – usually right before simmering point. Transfer to a bowl to cool, stirring every once in a while to prevent a skin from forming.

Once the custard has cooled, whip the cream into soft peaks, then fold into the custard to lighten it. Chill for a few hours or overnight, if preparing in advance.

To assemble the trifles, spoon the custard to fill the bottom third of 8 small clear glasses. Cut 4 attractive strawberries into quarters and set aside along with 8 small sprays of redcurrants. Put the rest into a large bowl along with the crème de cassis and a little icing sugar. Crush the fruit with a potato masher or a large fork to get a compote-like texture. Spoon a layer of this into each serving glass, then top with the remaining custard. If you have any left, spoon a little juice from the crushed fruit over the custards, then garnish with the reserved strawberry quarters and redcurrants.

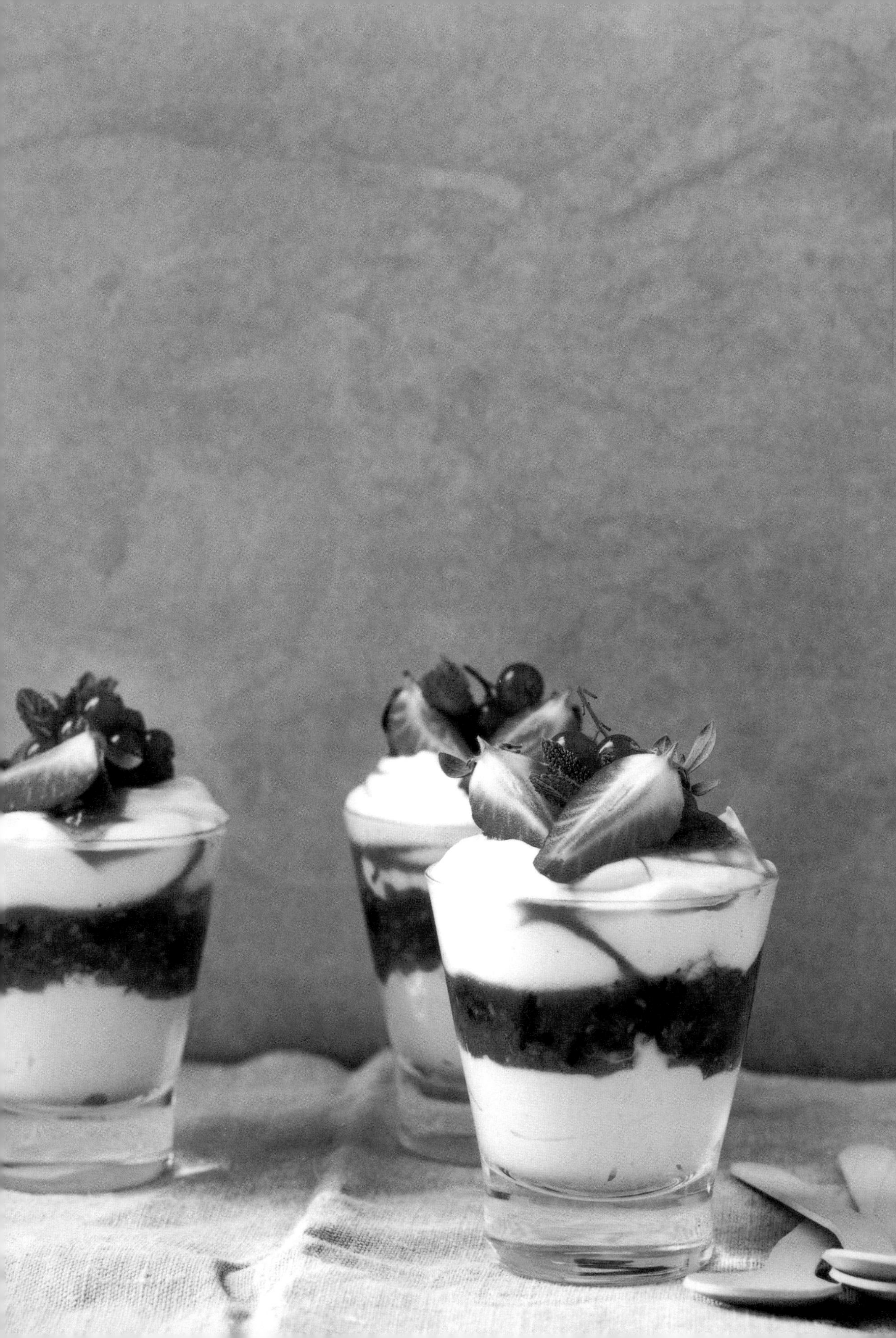

Peach, raspberry and ginger crumble

A little stem ginger lifts the flavours of the fruit in this crumble. The best way to eat it is warm from the oven, with a generous scoop of cold vanilla or ginger ice cream (see page 224).

SERVES 4–6
Filling:
butter, for greasing
8 firm but ripe peaches, about 750g
250g raspberries
2 tbsp lemon juice
2 tbsp crème de pêche (or icing sugar)
2 stem ginger in syrup, finely chopped

Crumble topping:
50g plain flour
pinch of fine sea salt
40g butter, diced
35g rolled oats
50g demerara sugar
½ tsp ground cinnamon
30g slivered almonds or crushed hazelnuts

Preheat the oven to 190°C/Gas 5. Lightly butter a wide 1.5-litre baking dish and set aside.

Halve the peaches, remove the stones and cut into wedges. Place in a large bowl and gently toss with the raspberries, lemon juice, crème de pêche and stem ginger. Spread the fruit evenly over the prepared baking dish and set aside.

To make the crumble topping, put the flour and salt into a bowl and add the diced butter. Rub the butter into the flour until the mixture resembles coarse breadcrumbs. Stir in the oats, sugar, cinnamon and nuts. Sprinkle the crumble evenly over the peaches and raspberries.

Bake for about 25–30 minutes until the topping is golden brown and the fruit underneath is soft. Remove and let stand for 10 minutes before serving.

Baked gooseberries with honey and almonds

Tart gooseberries need sugar and a touch of cream to balance out their acidity. This effortless recipe takes 10 or 15 minutes to make, and most of that time is spent topping and tailing the gooseberries. To say that gooseberries have a short season is an understatement. When not available, use thawed frozen gooseberries or substitute with other berries or stone fruits, such as plums or peaches.

Preheat the oven to 200°C/Gas 6 and lightly butter 4 individual baking dishes. Top and tail the gooseberries and divide among the baking dishes. Sprinkle with a little caster sugar, then scatter the almonds over and drizzle with a little honey. Dot a few small knobs of butter over the almonds and gooseberries.

Bake for 25–30 minutes until the gooseberries are soft and have started to burst. The almonds will be golden brown and caramelized. Remove the baking dishes from the oven and leave to cool slightly for a few minutes. Serve warm with a dollop of cold clotted cream.

SERVES 4
few knobs of butter
600g gooseberries
1–1½ tbsp caster sugar
50g flaked or nibbed almonds
runny honey, to drizzle
clotted cream, to serve

Fig ice cream

I've made this ice cream using black figs, and it comes out in a pretty shade of light purple. Creamy and luscious, the ice cream makes the perfect accompaniment to a pecan tart, or simply serve it with a bowl of fresh figs drizzled with honey.

Trim off the stems from the top of each fig and cut into eighths. Put the figs in a saucepan with the sugar, water and lemon zest. Cook over moderate heat, stirring frequently, for about 20 minutes until the liquid has reduced to a syrup and the figs have broken down to a jammy texture. Transfer to a wide bowl and leave to cool completely.

To make the ice cream base, put the cooked figs into a blender and pour in the cream and lemon juice to taste. Whiz until smooth and stop the machine once it starts to thicken and increase in volume. Scrape the mixture into an ice cream machine and churn until almost firm. Scoop into a suitable container and freeze until firm.

Remove the ice cream from the freezer for about 10–15 minutes to allow it to soften a little before serving.

SERVES 8
16 fresh figs in season
  (or about 8 dried ones)
125g caster sugar
125ml water
finely grated zest of
  1 lemon
600ml double cream
3–4 tbsp lemon juice

Cinnamon rice pudding with apricot compote

Rice pudding is pure comfort food. I really enjoy a bowl of warm rice pudding in the winter, and it is equally good served chilled in the summer, with fresh fruit compote. The pudding tends to set when cold, so loosen the consistency with a splash of milk or a little extra cream right before serving. Any extra compote would be great with breakfast muesli.

SERVES 6, WITH EXTRA COMPOTE

Rice pudding:
200g pudding rice
600ml whole milk
pinch of fine sea salt
100g caster sugar
1 cinnamon stick
200ml single cream,
    plus optional extra to serve

Apricot compote:
500g ripe apricots
25g unsalted butter
3–4 tbsp caster sugar
2 star anise
1 cinnamon stick

Put the rice, milk, salt, sugar and cinnamon into a heavy-based saucepan. Bring to the boil, stirring once or twice, then turn the heat to very low. Partially cover the pan with a lid and slowly simmer for about 45–55 minutes until the rice is tender. Remember to stir the pudding frequently or the rice will catch and burn at the bottom of the pan. Remove the pan from the heat and allow to stand for 5 minutes, then stir in the cream. Keep warm.

While the rice pudding is cooking, halve and stone the apricots, then roughly chop them up. Melt the butter in a pan and tip in the apricots, sugar, star anise and cinnamon. Toss over high heat for 3–4 minutes, just until the apricots are soft. Tip into a bowl and leave to cool slightly.

To serve, spoon the warm rice pudding into individual serving bowls or glasses, then top each with a generous spoonful of the apricot compote.

Custard tart

A few orange zests lend a mild fragrance to this custard tart. As it is not overly sweet but high in calcium-rich dairy, I think it's a good pudding to serve to children as a teatime treat. My lot can devour this in minutes.

Roll out the pastry on a lightly floured surface to about the thickness of a £1 coin. Use it to line a 23–25cm wide, 3–4cm deep tart tin with removable base. Press the pastry into the corners of the tin and leave a little excess overhanging the sides. Chill for at least 30 minutes.

Preheat the oven to 190°C/Gas 5. Line the pastry tin with foil and baking beans. Bake blind for 15–20 minutes until the pastry is firm and lightly golden round the edges. Remove the foil and beans and return to the oven for another 5 minutes until the base is cooked through and you don't see any uncooked patches. Remove and cool slightly. Lower the oven temperature to 150°C/Gas 2.

While the pastry is cooling, prepare the custard. Put the milk, cream, orange zest, and vanilla pod and seeds into a saucepan and bring to a simmer. Beat the sugar and egg yolks together in a large bowl. As soon as the creamy milk begins to scald, slowly trickle it into the egg mixture, stirring continuously as you do. When fully incorporated, strain the mixture and discard the orange zest and vanilla pod.

Trim the edges of the pastry level with the rim. Put the pastry case into the oven and pull out the oven shelf halfway so that the tin is still level. Pour in the custard until it almost reaches the top and carefully slide the oven shelf back. Bake for about 30–40 minutes until the custard is set but still has a slight wobble in the centre. Remove from the oven and dust the surface with freshly grated nutmeg. Cool completely before slicing with a sharp serrated knife.

SERVES 8

**300g sweet flan pastry
(see page 263)**
300ml whole milk
300ml double cream
**3 pared strips of
orange zest**
**1 vanilla pod, split
lengthways and seeds
scraped**
60g caster sugar
6 large egg yolks
fresh nutmeg, to grate

Lemon meringue pie

I loved lemon meringue pie as a child, but now I'm a little less keen on the texture of the lemon cornflour filling. My version uses a rich French-style lemon tart as the base, which is then topped with a generous pile of pillowy white meringue. Irresistible. (Illustrated on page 217.)

(Illustrated on page 217.)

SERVES 6
300g sweet flan pastry (see page 263)

Lemon filling:
juice of 2 lemons
175g caster sugar
6 large egg yolks
250ml double cream

Meringue:
175g caster sugar
4 large egg whites

Roll out the pastry on a lightly floured surface to about the thickness of a £1 coin and use to line a 20cm tart tin with removable base. Press the pastry well into the edges and leave a little excess overhanging the edge. Chill for at least 30 minutes.

Preheat the oven to 190°C/Gas 5. Line the pastry with foil and fill with baking beans. Bake for 15–20 minutes until the edges are lightly golden. Remove the foil and beans and bake for another 5 minutes until the base is cooked. Allow to cool, then trim the pastry level with the rim. Reduce the oven temperature to 140°C/Gas 1.

Whisk together all the ingredients for the filling, taking care not to aerate the mixture too much. Put the pastry case on the middle shelf of the oven and pull the shelf out halfway so that the tin is still level. Pour in the filling and carefully slide the shelf back. Bake for about 30 minutes, just until the filling looks lightly set. Turn off the oven and leave the tart inside to cool slowly. It will continue to set as it cools. Take the tart out of the oven only when it has completely cooled, after a few hours or overnight.

For best results, make the meringue just 10–15 minutes before you are ready to serve. Preheat the grill to the highest setting. Toss the sugar in a pan over low heat. You do not want to melt the sugar, just heat it until it is warm to the touch. (The warmth of the sugar helps to stabilize the beaten egg whites.) Beat the egg whites to stiff peaks in a grease-free bowl. Gradually beat in the warm sugar, a little at a time, and continue beating until the egg whites return to firm peaks. When all the sugar has been incorporated, the meringue should have tripled in volume and will be firm and glossy.

Spread the meringue over the tart and grill for 2–3 minutes until browned around the edges. Alternatively, run a blowtorch over the meringue until nicely caramelized.

Bakewell tart

At the Cobweb tearooms in Stratford-upon-Avon, where my mother used to work when I was a kid, they had a German pastry chef who produced beautiful continental-style cakes and pastries. One day, Mum took in a tray of her Bakewell tarts. I still remember the beaming smile on her face as she came home with the empty tray, having sold the lot. The best tarts are made with home-made strawberry jam. With store-bought jam, taste it first, reducing the amount if too sweet.

Roll out the pastry on a lightly floured surface to about the thickness of a £1 coin, then use most of it to line a 23–25cm-wide, 4cm-deep fluted tart tin with a removable base. Leave a little excess pastry sticking up above the tin. Chill for 30 minutes while you preheat the oven to 190°C/Gas 5. Meanwhile, re-roll the pastry trimmings into a rough rectangle and transfer to a baking sheet. Use a ruler as a guide to cut out neat 1cm strips. These will be used to decorate the tart. Chill.

Line the pastry tin with foil and fill with baking beans. Bake blind for 15–20 minutes until the pastry is firm and lightly golden round the edges. Remove the foil and beans and return to the oven for another 5 minutes until the base is golden and you don't see any uncooked patches. Take the pastry out of the oven to cool slightly and turn the oven down to 180°C/Gas 4.

For the topping, beat the butter and sugar together until light and fluffy. Gradually beat in the eggs and vanilla, then fold through the ground almonds and flour. Trim off the excess pastry from the cooked shell. Spoon a thin layer of strawberry jam over the base of the pastry, then spread the almond mixture over the jam. Use the pastry strips to create a lattice pattern on top of the filling, leaving a couple of centimetres' gap between the strips, then trim off any ends that stick out. Bake for 35–40 minutes until the top is a light golden brown. Remove from the oven and leave to cool. While the tart is still warm, brush a little apricot glaze over the top. Allow to cool completely before slicing and serving.

SERVES 10–12
500g sweet flan pastry (see page 263)
300g unsalted butter, softened to room temperature
275g caster sugar
3 large eggs, lightly beaten
1 tsp vanilla extract
300g ground almonds
3 tbsp plain flour
3–4 tbsp strawberry jam, home-made or, if shop-bought, ideally choose a reduced-sugar variety
2 tbsp apricot jam, mixed with 1–2 tsp boiling water

Poached rhubarb with ginger ice cream

I love pink rhubarb. For me, it has to be lightly poached and still retain its shape. Then it needs to be paired with something creamy, and here ginger ice cream does the trick perfectly. (Illustrated on page 223.)

SERVES 4–6

Poached rhubarb:
400g rhubarb
250g caster sugar
500ml water
1 vanilla pod, split lengthways and seeds scraped

Ginger ice cream:
250ml whole milk
250ml double cream
15g fresh ginger, peeled and grated
6 large egg yolks
80g caster sugar
40g stem ginger in syrup, sliced into thin matchsticks (optional)

Trim the tops and ends of the rhubarb and cut diagonally into 3cm lengths. Put the sugar, water, and vanilla pod and seeds into a saucepan and stir over low heat until the sugar has dissolved. Increase the heat slightly and simmer for 2–3 minutes until the syrup has thickened slightly. Tip in the rhubarb and poach for 3–5 minutes until just tender but still holding its shape. Remove the rhubarb with a slotted spoon and put into a bowl.

Boil the syrup for 8–10 minutes until reduced by two-thirds to a syrupy sauce. Pour the sauce over the rhubarb, leave to cool completely, then chill. With time, the rhubarb will continue to stain the poaching syrup into a gorgeous pink sauce. The poached rhubarb can be kept chilled for up to 1 week.

For the ginger ice cream, put the milk, cream and grated ginger into a saucepan and bring to the boil. Meanwhile, beat the egg yolks and sugar together in a large heatproof bowl. When the milk and cream begin to bubble up the sides of the pan, remove from the heat. Slowly trickle the hot liquid into the egg and sugar mixture, stirring continuously. When fully incorporated, strain the combined mixture into a clean saucepan. Return to a low heat and stir constantly until the mixture thickens to a custard. It should lightly coat the back of a wooden spoon.

Remove from the heat and stir in the stem ginger, if using. Leave to cool completely, giving the custard a stir every now and then to prevent a skin from forming. Pour into the bowl of an ice cream machine and churn until almost firm. Transfer to a suitable container and freeze for at least 6 hours or overnight.

Take the ginger ice cream out of the freezer 5–10 minutes before serving to allow it to soften slightly. Serve neat scoops alongside the poached rhubarb and sauce.

Mixed berry tartlets with vanilla and peach cream

These gorgeous tartlets are great for indoor entertaining and they make fabulous desserts for picnics and barbecues, too. You need to take care when packing and transporting the delicate pastry shells: layer them in between sheets of greaseproof paper and/or kitchen paper in a sturdy airtight container. If you like, lay out bowls of the vanilla and peach cream and the mixed berries next to the pastry shells and let people assemble the tarts themselves. (Illustrated on page 226.)

SERVES 6, WITH EXTRA VANILLA CREAM
500g walnut pastry (see page 263)
450–500g mixed berries (such as blackberries, blueberries, wild strawberries and
    raspberries)
icing sugar, to dust

Vanilla and peach cream:
250ml whole milk
half a vanilla pod, split lengthways and seeds scraped
50g caster sugar
20g cornflour
3 large egg yolks
200ml double cream
1–2 tbsp crème de pêche, to taste

Have ready six 10cm tartlet tins with removable bases. Roll out the pastry on a lightly floured surface into a thick log. Divide the log into 6 equal pieces. Shape a piece into a round ball, flatten it with the palm of your hand and roll out into a thin circle. Gently press the dough into a tartlet tin and trim off the excess pastry. Repeat with the remaining dough. Put the tarts on a baking sheet and chill for about 30 minutes.

To make the vanilla cream, put the milk and vanilla pod and seeds into a saucepan with a tablespoon of sugar. Place the pan over high heat until the milk begins to boil. Meanwhile, mix together the remaining sugar and cornflour in a large bowl, then beat in the yolks until the mixture is smooth.

Just as the milk begins to scald, remove from the heat and gradually trickle into the egg mixture, stirring continuously to prevent the eggs from scrambling. When fully incorporated, rinse out the pan. Pass the mixture through a fine sieve into the clean pan and return to the heat. Slowly stir the mixture over low heat for a few minutes until it thickens to a thick custard. Sieve the custard again (if you like, to ensure extra smoothness) into a large, clean bowl. Stir occasionally as it cools to prevent a skin from forming.

Preheat the oven to 200°C/Gas 6. Line each tartlet with small pieces of foil or greaseproof paper and fill with baking beans. Place the tartlet tins on a baking sheet and bake for 10–12 minutes. Remove the baking beans and foil or greaseproof paper and return to the oven for another 5 minutes to finish cooking the bases. Leave to cool for 10 minutes, then unmould the pastry cases and cool on a wire rack.

Whip the cream to soft peaks. Beat the cooled vanilla custard slightly to loosen it, then fold in the cream and the crème de pêche to taste. Chill until ready to serve.

Pipe or spoon the vanilla cream into each pastry shell and top with a mixture of fresh berries. Dust with a little icing sugar and serve.

Blackberry sorbet with shortbread fingers

This blackberry sorbet takes minutes to make: lightly poach the blackberries in syrup, liquidize and strain, cool and churn. While waiting for the sorbet to churn, or after you've put it in the freezer, use the time to make shortbread fingers. You will make more shortbread fingers than you need, but the remainder will keep for a couple of weeks in an airtight tin.

SERVES 6–8, WITH EXTRA SHORTBREAD FINGERS

Blackberry sorbet:
225ml granulated sugar
250ml water
500g blackberries
2 tbsp lemon juice

Shortbread fingers:
125g unsalted butter, softened to room temperature
90g caster sugar
1 large egg, beaten
250g plain flour, sifted with ¼ tsp fine sea salt

First, make the sorbet. Put the sugar and water in a small saucepan and stir over low heat until the sugar has dissolved. Turn up the heat slightly and simmer for a few minutes. Tip in the blackberries and simmer for a couple more minutes.

Transfer the blackberries and syrup to a blender and process until smooth. Strain the mixture through a fine sieve and discard the seeds. Stir in the lemon juice and leave to cool completely. If you have time, chill the mixture for about an hour.

Put the sorbet mixture into the bowl of an ice cream machine and churn until almost firm. Transfer to a suitable container and freeze until solid.

For the shortbread, beat the butter and sugar in an electric mixer until smooth and creamy, then gradually work in the egg. Turn the machine to the slowest setting and mix in the flour, a spoonful at a time, until the dough just comes together. Press the dough together into a ball, wrap in cling film and chill for at least an hour to allow it to firm up.

Preheat the oven to 160°C/Gas 2. Roll out the dough to ½cm thickness. Use a long cook's knife or a palette knife to trim the edges to form a neat rectangle. Transfer the dough onto a baking sheet using a rolling pin, then mark out rectangles of 2cm x 9cm using a clean ruler and a long knife. Prick each rectangle a few times with a fork and sprinkle over a little caster sugar.

Bake for about 20–25 minutes until the dough turns a pale golden colour. Cool on the tray for half a minute, then cut along the scored sides to separate the fingers. Place on a wire rack to cool completely. Store in an airtight container until ready to serve.

Remove the sorbet from the freezer about 5–10 minutes before serving to allow it to soften slightly. Scoop into chilled serving glasses and serve with the shortbread fingers on the side.

chocolate
and coffee

When I worked in Paris as a humble commis chef at *Guy Savoy*, helping out in the pastry section, I took every opportunity to improve my pastry-, chocolate- and cake-making skills. To begin with, I got the simpler tasks: rolling hundreds of handmade chocolate truffles to serve with teas and coffees, for example. After several months of proving my aptitude and determination, I was finally allowed to make fantastic desserts on my own, many of which were exquisite chocolate creations.

Baking with chocolate is similar to cooking with wine. You get out what you put in. It always pays to use good-quality cooking chocolate with a high percentage of cocoa solids – the range for dark chocolate is usually between 65 and 72 per cent – particularly if chocolate is the dominant flavour in a dessert. Even if a recipe calls for plain or milk chocolate, spend a little more on buying the best quality.

Chocolate swirl cheesecake
Double chocolate parfait
Chocolate chip pancakes with orange brandy sauce
Sticky toffee and chocolate pudding
Chocolate and coffee pots
Black forest cake
Dark chocolate marquise
Coffee and almond crunch cake
Chocolate roulade with chocolate chestnut cream

Chocolate swirl cheesecake

This New-York-style cheesecake is rich, creamy and made a little more decadent by swirls of melted dark chocolate. To cut through the richness, serve with fresh fruit compote. The American tradition is to top the cheesecake with blueberry compote, but one made with a mixture of berries or other soft, tart fruit will also work nicely.

Preheat the oven to 170°C/Gas 3 and butter a 23cm round springform cake tin. Break the digestive biscuits into small pieces and place in the bowl of a food processor along with the almonds. Whiz to fine crumbs. Add the melted butter and pulse until the mixture comes together. Tip the mixture into the tin and press down with a spatula to form an even crust. Bake in the preheated oven for 10–15 minutes until golden.

Reduce the oven temperature to 140°C/Gas 1. Melt the dark chocolate in a heatproof bowl set over a pan of barely simmering water. Stir until the chocolate is smooth, then remove from the heat.

In a large mixing bowl, beat together the rest of the ingredients using a hand-held electric beater. Pour the cheesecake mixture into the cake tin and tap the tin gently to level the mixture and remove any large air bubbles. Swirl the melted dark chocolate on top.

Bake for about 30 minutes until the filling is set round the sides but the centre is still wobbly when you gently shake the pan. Turn off the heat and leave to cool slowly in the oven, preferably overnight. The cheesecake filling continues to set as it cools, and taking it out of the oven too soon may cause it to crack.

Take the cheesecake out of the springform tin and slide on to a serving plate or cake stand. Best served chilled.

SERVES 8–10
150g digestive biscuits
15g flaked almonds, toasted
60g unsalted butter, melted
75g dark chocolate (minimum 65% cocoa solids), roughly chopped
150g caster sugar
250ml sour cream
600g cream cheese
2 large eggs
1 tsp vanilla extract

Double chocolate parfait

Rich and luscious, this is the parfait with which to tempt chocolate-lovers. As I hardly need to tell you, use top-quality chocolate for both layers.

SERVES 8

100g dark chocolate (minimum 65% cocoa solids), chopped
150g plain cooking (or milk) chocolate, chopped
300ml double cream, lightly whipped
200g raspberries, to serve (optional)

Mousse base:
150g caster sugar
100ml water
5 large egg yolks

First, prepare the mousse base. Put the sugar and water in a small saucepan and stir over low heat to dissolve, then increase the heat and bring to the boil. Boil for about 7–10 minutes until the liquid is thick and syrupy. The temperature should register 110°C on a sugar thermometer.

While the sugar syrup is boiling, use a hand-held electric beater to whisk the egg yolks in a medium heatproof bowl until smooth and fluffy. Carefully and slowly trickle in the hot sugar syrup, whisking vigorously until the mixture is thick, glossy and tripled in volume. Continue to whisk for another 5 minutes until the mixture has cooled and the sides of the bowl no longer feel hot. Set aside.

Put the dark and plain chocolates into separate large heatproof bowls. One at a time, melt each chocolate in its bowl, set over a pan of barely simmering water. Stir the chocolate every once in a while until melted and smooth. Remove from the heat and leave to cool slightly. Meanwhile, whip the double cream to soft peaks.

Divide the mousse base between the two bowls of melted chocolate and fold through until evenly combined. Finally, fold half the whipped cream into each chocolate base.

Line a 900g loaf tin with a large sheet of cling film, with the excess hanging over the sides. Spread the dark chocolate mousse evenly over the base, filling in the corners. Make sure the tin is level, and freeze for a couple of hours until the top is firm. In the meantime, keep the plain chocolate mousse chilled. Remove the dark chocolate parfait from the freezer and spread the plain chocolate mixture on top to fill the tin. Cover the mousse with the excess cling film and freeze for at least 8 hours or overnight.

Remove the parfait from the freezer 5–10 minutes before serving to allow it to soften. Unmould from the loaf tin on to a clean chopping board and peel off the cling film. Cut into thick slices using a warm knife. Serve with a scattering of raspberries if you wish.

Chocolate chip pancakes with orange brandy sauce

For even more luxury, add a scoop of vanilla ice cream to the warm pancakes and brandy sauce, and serve straight away. Or to make a special breakfast treat, such as for a child's birthday, serve the chocolate chip pancakes with maple syrup instead of brandy sauce.

SERVES 5–6

Chocolate chip pancakes:
100g plain flour
1 tsp baking powder
pinch of fine sea salt
150ml buttermilk
2 large eggs, separated
50ml cold water
50g chocolate chips
few knobs of butter, for frying

Orange brandy sauce:
50g dark chocolate, roughly chopped
120ml single cream
2 tbsp caster sugar
1 tbsp brandy or Grand Marnier/Cointreau
2 tbsp orange juice
orange segments, to garnish (optional)

To make the pancakes, sift the flour, baking powder and salt into a large mixing bowl and make a well in the middle. In a separate bowl, whisk the buttermilk, egg yolks and water together, then pour into the well. Gradually incorporate the flour into the wet ingredients until you have a smooth and lump-free batter. Whisk the egg whites to firm peaks, then fold into the pancake batter.

Cook the pancakes in batches of 2 or 3. Heat a wide non-stick frying pan with a knob of butter. Pour a small ladleful of the batter into the pan for each pancake, then drop a few chocolate chips over the top. Fry for a minute until golden brown underneath, then flip over and cook the other side for a further 45 seconds to a minute. The pancakes should puff up as they cook. Keep them warm in a low oven while you cook the rest.

For the sauce, place the chocolate, cream and sugar in a small saucepan. Set the pan over low heat and stir until the chocolate and sugar have melted and the sauce is smooth. Stir in the brandy and orange juice, then pour into a warm serving jug.

Pile the pancakes on warm plates and drizzle with the sauce. Garnish with orange segments if you wish.

Sticky toffee and chocolate pudding

I can't resist a good sticky toffee pudding. For me, this is the perfect ending to a meal on a cold, wintry day. It pays to use medjool dates here, as their toffee-like flavour adds depth to the pudding.

Preheat the oven to 190°C/Gas 5. Butter, line and butter again 8 175–200ml pudding basins. (Or use a 1-litre basin to make one large pudding.)

Put the dates, sugar and water in a saucepan and simmer gently for 10 minutes until the sugar has dissolved and the dates are soft. Leave to cool, then blend in a food processor until smooth. Add the butter, vanilla, espresso and eggs and whiz again until well blended. Scrape the mixture into a large mixing bowl. In 2 batches, sift the flour, cocoa powder, bicarbonate of soda and baking powder over the bowl and fold into the wet mixture. Divide among the prepared basins and bake for 20–25 minutes (or 50–60 minutes if using a large basin). The puddings are ready when a skewer emerges fairly clean when inserted into the centre.

Put all the sauce ingredients into a saucepan and simmer, stirring frequently, until the butter and sugar have dissolved and the sauce is smooth. It should only take 2–3 minutes. Keep warm and give it a stir every once in a while to prevent a skin from forming on top.

When the puddings are just cool enough to handle, but still warm, run a small knife along the sides, then invert on to individual serving bowls. Peel off the baking parchment. Pour a generous drizzle of warm toffee sauce over the puddings and serve immediately, with a jug of pouring cream to hand around.

SERVES 8

Pudding:
- 200g medjool dates, pitted and chopped
- 175g dark muscovado sugar
- 250ml water
- 100g lightly salted butter, softened
- 1 tsp vanilla extract
- 1 tbsp cooled espresso or strong coffee
- 3 large eggs
- 150g plain flour
- 50g cocoa powder
- 1 tsp bicarbonate of soda
- 1 tsp baking powder
- pouring cream, to serve

Toffee sauce:
- 100g dark muscovado sugar
- 75g lightly salted butter
- 250ml double cream

Chocolate and coffee pots

These chocolate and coffee custards are rich and meltingly smooth, and as good on the eye as they are on the palate. Because the custards are gently baked in a water bath, you can set them in pretty teacups, as I have done, or use regular ramekins for a simpler presentation.

Preheat the oven to 170°C/Gas 3. In a medium saucepan, heat the cream until just beginning to simmer, then add the chocolate and stir until the chocolate has melted and the mixture is smooth. Remove the pan from the heat, stir in the single cream and leave to cool.

Bring a kettle of water to the boil. Using an electric beater, whisk the egg yolks and sugar in a bowl until pale and thick enough to fall from the whisk in a lazy ribbon: about 5 minutes. Fold in the chocolate cream, followed by the espresso.

Divide the mixture among 4 individual 125–150ml ramekins or ceramic pots. Place the filled pots into a deep baking tray. Put the tray on the bottom shelf of the oven and pull out the shelf halfway while keeping the pan level. Carefully pour in enough boiling water to come halfway up the sides of the pots and push the shelf back in. Bake for about 20–25 minutes until just set at the edges. They should be slightly soft in the centre when ready.

Remove the pots from the water bath and cool completely. Chill for a few hours or overnight. Remove from the refrigerator 10–15 minutes before serving, with a neat little dollop of crème fraiche and some chocolate shavings if you like.

SERVES 4
200ml double cream
100g dark chocolate
   (minimum 65% cocoa
   solids), chopped
50ml single cream
2 large egg yolks
30g caster sugar
2 tbsp cooled espresso
   or strong coffee
4 tbsp crème fraiche,
   to serve (optional)
chocolate shavings,
   to garnish (optional)

Black forest cake

Some retro desserts, such as black forest gateau, have seen a revival over the past few years. It's no surprise: dark chocolate and cherries will always be a winning combination. The chocolate sponge in this recipe has just the right texture for absorbing a drizzle of kirsch, which keeps it delectably moist. Fresh stemmed cherries are the perfect garnish for the assembled cake, but if they're not available, use a large jar of marinated cherries in kirsch. (Illustrated on page 244.)

SERVES 8

Chocolate sponge:
125g self-raising flour
2 tsp baking powder
3 tbsp cocoa powder
5 large eggs, separated
200g unsalted butter, softened
150g caster sugar
2 tbsp cooled espresso or strong coffee
100g dark chocolate (minimum 65% cocoa solids),
    melted in a bowl set over a pan of simmering water

Filling and topping:
500g ripe cherries
60g caster sugar
75ml kirsch or cherry brandy
550ml double cream
1–2 tbsp icing sugar, to taste
4–5 tbsp good-quality cherry compote
grated chocolate, to garnish

Preheat the oven to 150°C/Gas 2. Butter, line and butter again the base and sides of a 23cm cake tin. Sieve the flour, baking powder and cocoa powder together and set aside.

In a large grease-free bowl, whisk the egg whites to firm peaks using an electric beater. Beat the butter and sugar in another mixing bowl until pale and light. Beat in the yolks one at a time, then fold the espresso through, followed by the melted chocolate.

In several batches, fold the sifted flour mixture and the beaten egg whites alternately into the butter mixture. Spread the combined batter over the base of the prepared tin and level with a spatula. Bake for 40–50 minutes until a skewer inserted into the middle of the cake emerges clean. Cool for 5 minutes and then turn out on to a wire rack. Peel off the baking parchment.

Remove the stems and pit three-quarters of the cherries, leaving the stems on the remaining cherries to garnish. Put all the cherries, the sugar and kirsch in a saucepan and bring to a simmer. Simmer until the cherries are just soft, giving them an occasional stir. Tip the cherries and kirsch syrup into a bowl and leave to cool completely. Meanwhile, whisk the cream and icing sugar into soft peaks.

Using a long, sharp knife, halve the cake horizontally. Drizzle each half with the kirsch syrup from the cherries to moisten. Place the bottom half on a cake stand and spread over half the whipped cream. Arrange the stemmed and pitted cherries over the cream, then spoon over a layer of cherry compote. Top with the upper half of the cake. Spread the remaining cream on top. Sprinkle over a little grated chocolate, then garnish with the whole stemmed cherries. Best served on the day it is made.

Dark chocolate marquise

There's no denying this is a seriously rich and indulgent pudding. When you take a bite, the velvety smooth mousse melts in your mouth. It requires a bit of patience and persistence to make – you need to whisk separated eggs and cream individually, then fold together with melted dark chocolate. I've set the mousse on top of a thin chocolate sponge base, which you could replace with a simple cheesecake base (see page 235). (Illustrated on page 249.)

SERVES 12
Sponge base:
3 medium eggs, separated
75g caster sugar
30g cornflour
20g cocoa powder
30g plain flour

Rich mousse topping:
300g dark chocolate (minimum 65% cocoa solids), roughly chopped
2 tbsp Grand Marnier/Cointreau, plus extra to drizzle
2 tbsp orange juice
3 large eggs
30g caster sugar
3 tbsp runny honey
300ml double cream
cocoa powder, to dust

First, make the sponge base. Preheat the oven to 200°C/Gas 6. Line a baking sheet with a large sheet of baking parchment. Whisk the egg whites in a large mixing bowl until just firm. Gradually beat in the sugar until you get a stiff meringue. Beat the egg yolks in a different bowl until light and fluffy, then fold into the egg white mixture.

Sift the cornflour, cocoa powder and flour together over the mixture and fold through. Spread the mixture over the lined baking sheet to a large round, approximately 25–30cm in diameter. Don't worry if it is not a perfect circle, just as long as it is even in thickness. Bake for 7–8 minutes until the sponge is set and springy when pressed. Invert on to a wire rack to cool and peel off the baking parchment.

For the mousse topping, melt the chocolate in a large heatproof bowl set over a pan of barely simmering water. Remove the bowl from the heat and leave to cool slightly, then fold in the Grand Marnier and orange juice. Let the pan of water continue to simmer over very low heat.

Use a hand-held electric beater to whisk the eggs in a large heatproof bowl. When the eggs are light and fluffy, add the sugar and honey, then place the bowl over the pan of barely simmering water. Whisk for about 5–10 minutes until the mixture is light, fluffy and has more than tripled in volume. Remove the bowl from the pan and continue to whisk until it has cooled slightly.

Using the same beaters, whisk the cream to soft peaks. Fold into the egg mixture. Finally, fold in the melted chocolate until well incorporated.

Use a 25cm springform cake tin as a guide to cut out a neat circle from the sponge base, then use this to line the base of the tin. Drizzle a few tablespoons of Grand Marnier over the base, then spread the chocolate mousse mixture on top. Level the top with a spatula or palette knife. Chill for at least 6 hours or overnight until set. Dust the top with cocoa powder, then unmould and cut into individual slices using a warm knife.

Coffee and almond crunch cake

For me, this is the definitive cake to have with coffee or tea. It is all-at-once tender, moist and crunchy. It keeps well for several days in a cool part of the kitchen. Some people like a dollop of lightly sweetened mascarpone on the side, though, for me, it's perfect on its own.

SERVES 6–8

Cake:
170g unsalted butter
170g caster sugar
3 large eggs, lightly beaten
½ tsp almond essence
100g ground almonds
4 tbsp cooled espresso or strong coffee
100g self-raising flour
½ tsp baking powder
icing sugar, to dust

Crunch topping:
60g plain flour
40g light brown or demerara sugar
40g cold unsalted butter, diced

Preheat the oven to 150°C/Gas 2. Butter and line the sides and base of a tall-sided 20cm cake tin with a removable base. For the crunch topping, mix the flour and sugar in a bowl and rub in the butter until it resembles coarse breadcrumbs. Set aside.

Cream the butter and sugar in a large mixing bowl using a hand-held electric beater until light and fluffy. Beat in the eggs, a little at a time, until fully incorporated. Add the almond essence and mix well. Fold in the ground almonds, followed by half the espresso. Sift in the flour and baking powder together and fold this through the wet mixture. Finally, fold in the remaining espresso.

Spread the mixture into the cake tin and level with a spatula. Sprinkle the crunch topping evenly over the top. Bake for 50–60 minutes until the top is golden brown and a skewer inserted into the cake comes out clean. Remove from the oven and leave to cool slightly before unmoulding on to a wire rack, peeling away the baking parchment. When completely cooled, dust with icing sugar, then cut into slices to serve.

Chocolate roulade with chocolate chestnut cream

The creamy chestnut filling goes perfectly with the light chocolate sponge in this dessert. It's also good to offer at teatime, and you could even dress it up into a Christmas log with chocolate frosting (or simply dust with icing sugar) and chocolate leaves.

SERVES 8–10
Chocolate sponge:
icing sugar, to dust
cocoa powder, to dust
5 large egg whites
150g caster sugar
25g self-raising flour
100g dark chocolate (minimum 65% cocoa solids),
   melted in a bowl set over a pan of simmering water
3 tbsp cooled espresso or strong coffee

Filling:
250g sweetened chestnut purée
100g dark chocolate (minimum 65% cocoa solids),
   melted in a bowl set over a pan of simmering water
200ml double cream

Preheat the oven to 190°C/Gas 5. Lightly oil and line a Swiss roll tin or large roasting tin, about 25 x 35cm, with baking parchment, leaving the edges sticking up around the sides. Dust evenly with a mixture of icing sugar and cocoa powder (about a tablespoon of each mixed together).

Whisk the egg whites to stiff peaks in a large grease-free bowl using a hand-held electric beater. Gradually whisk in the sugar, a tablespoon at a time, and return to firm peaks. Sift the flour over the meringue and fold through with a large metal spoon. Mix the melted chocolate with the espresso, then fold this through the meringue to combine. Spread the mixture on the baking parchment, using a palette knife to even out the surface. Bake for 15–20 minutes until the top is set and the sponge is slightly springy when pressed. Pull the parchment and slide the cake on to a wire rack to cool slightly. Cover with a damp tea towel and leave to cool completely.

Lay out a sheet of greaseproof paper, larger than the dimension of the sponge, and sieve over a little icing sugar and cocoa powder. Invert the sponge on top, then peel off the baking parchment that you used for cooking.

Mix together the chestnut purée and melted chocolate until smooth. Whip the cream until thick, then fold into the chocolate and chestnut mixture. Spread the chocolate and chestnut cream over the chocolate sponge, leaving 2cm clear around the edge.

Roll over the long edge of the sponge to form a neat log, using the parchment to help you. Making sure the seam-side of the log is underneath, wrap the parchment round it and then chill for at least an hour. If necessary, gently roll the roulade on a work surface to even out the shape, then unwrap and slide on to a cake stand. If you like, dust with icing sugar before slicing and serving.

basics

A good stock is the basis for many a successful dish. Making your own gives you more control over the finished dish, and allows you to make good use of trimmings and capture flavours that would otherwise be wasted. Stocks keep well in the freezer. Another home-made treat is mayonnaise: it tastes brilliant and is easy and quick to do. Abandon any idea you may have that making it is tricky. Making pastry is a little trickier, but it gets easier with practice. The only pastry I rarely make myself is puff pastry; I usually buy it from a good source. All the others, however, can be put together fairly simply, and the results always justify the small amount of work put in. This is my collection of essential basic recipes to enhance the dishes in this book.

Mayonnaise
Chicken stock & clear chicken stock
Vegetable stock
Beef stock
Lamb stock
Fish stock
Shortcrust pastry
Sweet flan pastry
Sweet walnut pastry & walnut and parmesan pastry

Mayonnaise

Makes about 600ml

4 large egg yolks
2 tsp white wine vinegar
2 tsp English mustard
600ml groundnut oil (or light olive oil)
1–2 tbsp cold water

Put the egg yolks, vinegar, mustard and some salt and pepper into a food processor and whiz until the mixture is very thick and creamy. With the motor running, slowly trickle in the oil in a steady stream. Add the water and whiz to help stabilize the emulsion. Taste and adjust the seasoning. Transfer to a jar, cover and chill for up to 3 days.

Chicken stock

Makes about 1.5 litres

2 tbsp olive oil
1 large carrot, roughly chopped
1 onion, roughly chopped
2 celery stalks, roughly chopped
1 leek, sliced
1 bay leaf
1 thyme sprig
3 garlic cloves, peeled
2 tbsp tomato purée
1kg raw chicken bones (roasted, if making brown chicken stock)

Heat the olive oil in a large stockpot and add the vegetables, herbs and garlic. Sauté over a medium heat, stirring occasionally, until the vegetables are golden. Stir in the tomato purée and cook for another minute. Add the chicken bones and then pour in enough cold water to cover: about 2 litres. Season lightly with salt and pepper. Bring to the boil and skim off any scum that rises to the surface. Reduce the heat and leave to simmer gently for 1 hour.

Let the stock stand for a few minutes to cool slightly and allow the ingredients to settle before passing through a fine sieve. Leave to cool and chill, or freeze in convenient portions. Use up fresh stock within 5 days or keep frozen for up to 3 months.

Clear chicken stock

Make the stock as above, strain and leave to cool completely. Liquidize 200g of minced chicken meat and 3 egg whites together in a food processor. Whisk the mixture into the stock and place over high heat. Keep whisking until the mixture comes to the boil. A foamy layer of impurities will float to the surface of the stock and form a crust. As soon as the liquid begins to creep up the sides of the pan, remove the pan from the heat. Carefully pour the stock through a muslin-lined sieve set over a large pot and let the liquid drip through. To keep the stock clear, do not press down on the crust or squeeze the muslin. Season to taste, and reheat the stock before serving.

Vegetable stock
Makes about 1.5 litres

3 onions, roughly chopped
1 leek, roughly chopped
2 celery stalks, roughly chopped
6 carrots, roughly chopped
1 head of garlic, split horizontally
1 tsp white peppercorns
1 bay leaf
few thyme, basil, tarragon, coriander and
        parsley sprigs, tied together
200ml dry white wine

Put the vegetables, garlic, peppercorns and bay leaf in a large stockpot and pour in cold water to cover: about 2 litres. Bring to the boil, lower the heat to a simmer and leave to cook gently for 20 minutes. Remove the pan from the heat and add the bundle of herbs, white wine and a little seasoning. Give the stock a stir and leave to cool completely.

If you have time, chill the stock overnight before straining. Pass the liquid through a fine sieve. Refrigerate and use within 5 days, or freeze the stock in convenient portions for up to 3 months.

Beef stock
Makes about 1.5 litres

1.5kg beef or veal marrowbones, chopped
        into 5–6cm pieces
2 tbsp olive oil, plus extra to drizzle
2 onions, roughly chopped
2 carrots, roughly chopped
2 celery stalks, roughly chopped
1 large fennel bulb, roughly chopped
1 tbsp tomato purée
100g button mushrooms
1 bay leaf
1 thyme sprig
1 tsp black peppercorns

Preheat the oven to 220°C/Gas 7. Spread the bones out in a large roasting tin and drizzle with a little olive oil to coat. Roast for about an hour, turning over halfway, until evenly browned.

Heat the oil in a large stockpot and add the vegetables. Stir occasionally over high heat until golden brown. Add the tomato purée and fry for another 2 minutes. Add the browned bones to the pan and pour in water to cover: about 2–2.5 litres. Bring to a simmer and skim off the froth and scum that rises to the surface.

Add the mushrooms, bay leaf, thyme and peppercorns. Simmer the stock for 6–8 hours until you are satisfied with the flavour. Let stand for a few minutes before passing through a fine sieve. Leave to cool and chill, or freeze in convenient portions. Use fresh stock within 5 days or keep frozen for up to 3 months.

Lamb stock

Makes about 1.2 litres

1kg lamb rib or neck bones
2–3 tbsp olive oil, plus extra to drizzle
1 onion, roughly chopped
2 carrots, roughly chopped
1 celery stalk, roughly chopped
half a head of garlic, horizontally split
1½ tsp tomato purée
75ml dry white wine
1 tsp black peppercorns
1 bay leaf
few sprigs of thyme and flat-leaf parsley

Preheat the oven to 220°C/Gas 7. Spread the bones out in a large roasting tin and drizzle with a little olive oil to coat. Roast for about 45–60 minutes, turning over halfway, until evenly browned.

Heat the oil in a large stockpot and add the vegetables and garlic. Stir occasionally over high heat until golden brown. Add the tomato purée and fry for another 2 minutes. Add the wine and let it boil until reduced by half. Add the browned bones to the pan. Pour in water to cover: about 2 litres. Bring to a simmer and skim off the froth and scum that rises to the surface.

Add the peppercorns and herbs. Simmer the stock for 4–6 hours until you are happy with the flavour, then take the pot off the heat. Let stand for a few minutes before passing through a fine sieve. Leave to cool and chill, or freeze in convenient portions. Use fresh stock within 5 days or keep frozen for up to 3 months.

Fish stock

Makes about 1 litre

1kg white fish bones and trimmings
2 tbsp olive oil
1 small onion, roughly chopped
half a celery stalk, roughly chopped
1 small fennel bulb, roughly chopped
1 small leek, sliced
75ml dry white wine

If using fish heads, cut out the eyes and gills and remove any traces of blood. Heat the olive oil in a stockpot and add the vegetables and a little salt and pepper. Stir over a medium heat for 3–4 minutes until the vegetables begin to soften but not brown. Add the fish bones and trimmings and the wine, and enough cold water to cover: about 1–1.2 litres. Simmer for 20 minutes, then remove from the heat and leave to cool.

Ladle the stock through a fine sieve and discard the solids. Refrigerate and use within 2 days or freeze in convenient portions for up to 3 months.

Shortcrust pastry
Makes about 450g

225g plain flour
1 tsp fine sea salt
150g cold unsalted butter, diced
4–6 tbsp ice-cold water
1 medium free-range egg, beaten

Place the flour and salt in a food processor. Add the butter and whiz for about 10 seconds until the mixture resembles coarse breadcrumbs. Tip into a mixing bowl. Add 4 tablespoons of water and stir the mixture with a butter knife until the dough just comes together. If it seems too dry, add another 1–2 tablespoons of water. (Try not to make the dough too wet, as it results in a crumbly pastry.) Lightly knead the dough into a smooth ball, wrap in cling film and chill for at least 30 minutes before using.

Sweet flan pastry
Makes about 500g

125g unsalted butter, softened to room
    temperature
90g caster sugar
1 large egg
250g plain flour

Place the butter and sugar in a food processor and whiz until just combined. Add the egg and whiz for 30 seconds. Tip in the flour and process for a few seconds until the dough just comes together. (Be careful not to over-process, or the dough will become tough.) Add a tablespoon of cold water if the dough seems too dry. Knead lightly on a floured surface and shape into a flat disc. Wrap in cling film and chill for 30 minutes before using.

Sweet walnut pastry
Makes about 500g

200g plain flour, sifted
100g finely ground walnuts
100g caster sugar
100g cold unsalted butter, diced
1 medium egg, lightly beaten
1–2 tbsp whole milk, to bind

Put the flour, walnuts and sugar into a food processor and pulse for a few seconds to mix. Add the cold butter and whiz into fine crumbs. Tip in the egg and pulse until the mixture comes together, adding a little milk, as necessary, to form a dough. Tip the dough onto a lightly floured surface and knead gently. Wrap in cling film and chill for at least 30 minutes before using.

Walnut and parmesan pastry
As above, but replace the caster sugar with 20g finely grated parmesan and a pinch of fine sea salt.

index

Page numbers in *italic* refer to recipes with finished-dish illustrations.

Acknowledgements

Where would I be without the tremendous amount of support that I receive from my teams? For this book, my team comprises Mark Sargeant, my right-hand man, who has worked on most of my books and helps to make sure that all is running smoothly; Emily Quah, for her invaluable work on the recipes and text; Ditte Isager, for her unique and stunning photography – it absolutely blew me away!; Patrick Budge and Christine Rudolph, for their creativity and for making the book so gorgeous and stylish; Viv Bowler, Mari Roberts and Lucy Deegan Leirião, for their thorough work on editing; and last but not least, Belinda Budge, for her support and for putting together an amazing team.

Many thanks also to my team at Head Office and the wonderful teams at the restaurants and pubs. Finally, thanks to the 'team' at home, for always being there.